VOLUME 90 • NUMBER 3 • FALL 2001

NATIO

CIVIC

REVIEW

MAKING CITIZEN DEMOCRACY WORK

IN THIS ISSUE

Digital Democracy: Civic Engagement in the Twenty-First Century

Christopher T. Gates
President, National Civic League

Robert Loper
Editor

A Publication of the National Civic League and Jossey-Bass

NATIONAL CIVIC REVIEW (ISSN 0027-9013) is published quarterly by Jossey-Bass, 989 Market Street, San Francisco, CA 94103-1741, and the National Civic League, 1445 Market Street, Suite 300, Denver, CO 80202-1717. NCL, founded in 1894 as the National Municipal League, advocates a new civic agenda to create communities that work for everyone. NCL is a 501(c)(3) nonprofit, nonpartisan educational association of individuals and organizations. NCL members have access to the information and services necessary to improve community life. For complete information, contact Derek Okubo, (303) 571-4343.

INDEXED in Public Affairs Information Service, ABC POL SCI, and Book Review Index.

SUBSCRIPTIONS are $55.00 per year for individuals and $105.00 per year for institutions. To order subscriptions, single issues, or reprints, please refer to the Ordering Information page at the back of this issue.

PERIODICALS postage paid at San Francisco, California, and at additional mailing offices. POSTMASTER: send address changes to National Civic Review, Jossey-Bass, 989 Market Street, San Francisco, CA 94103-1741.

NCL MEMBERS send change of address to Debbie Gettings, National Civic League, 1445 Market Street, Suite 300, Denver, CO 80202-1717.

EDITORIAL CORRESPONDENCE should be sent to Robert Loper, National Civic League, 1319 F Street NW, Suite 204, Washington DC, 20004.

www.josseybass.com

ISBN 978-0-7879-5820-6

LETTERS TO THE EDITOR. *National Civic Review* welcomes letters to the editor. Write to *National Civic Review,* 1319 F Street, Suite 204, Washington, DC, 20004, or send e-mail to robert@ncldc.org. Please include your name, address, and telephone number.

CONTENTS

In This Issue: Digital Democracy: Civic Engagement in the Twenty-First Century

ARTICLES

> Cyberspace bears a resemblance to the commons of medieval England or American colonial society. In both settings, shared stewardship generates social capital. However, left unchecked, modern "enclosure" movements may fence in the virtual frontier.

> Public libraries are on the front line, bridging the digital divide and wiring communities for civic engagement. Across the country, innovative programs leveraging support from foundations and the public and private sectors are helping individuals and communities become e-literate.

> The forms and processes of representative democracy may change as the irresistible force of Internet access meets the unmovable object of American government. To date, however, the encounter has largely complemented rather than revolutionized existing practices.

> E-government has the potential to make the relationship between citizens and government more citizen-centric. It is essential that normative concerns, including trust and equity, inform the process whereby digital democracy takes shape.

> The move from paper-based transactions to digitized operations will result in tremendous efficiencies throughout all levels of government. It will also increase citizen access and change existing forms of civic participation. This article takes a look ahead to the transformations in government structure that the virtual state may entail.

NOTE FROM THE PRESIDENT

The cooling off of the dot com economy ends a phase in the trajectory that information technology (IT) has been blazing across our society. Like a booster rocket propelling a satellite into orbit, speculative mania and turbocharged rhetoric fueled an explosive growth in IT. Although this wild ride is now literally and figuratively spent, its positive effects can be seen in the widespread adoption and implementation of information-based technologies in all sectors of society.

Looking past the current disarray in the high-tech industry, we can begin to assess more clearly the force these technologies exert on the direction of our society. One of the most telling indicators of this influence is how remote in time the pre-Internet world seems. We now take for granted the ability to search for information and make purchases at the click of a mouse. As anyone who has switched from a modem to DSL access can testify, in this new world there is simply no going back.

Information-based technologies have great promise for transforming far more than how Americans shop or surf for news and entertainment. The ease and rapidity with which information can be collected, stored, searched, and transmitted creates new opportunities and raises new concerns. On the one hand, barriers to participation in the political process can be dramatically lowered, keeping citizens informed and engaged; at the local level, greater community involvement can be encouraged through means such as neighborhood listservs and e-mail alerts. On the other hand, there are a number of serious questions concerning privacy safeguards, the openness of the Internet, and the ultimate impact of IT on our form of government.

For this reason, the National Civic League has again chosen to focus its annual conference on the interaction between IT and civic engagement. This year's national conference on governance, titled Digital Democracy: Civic Engagement in the Twenty-First Century, evaluates how the expanding use of information-based technologies is affecting politics, government, and community building.

The articles in this issue of the journal complement the focus of the conference. Although a range of themes are discussed, all of the articles relate to the ongoing development of digital democracy, or "e-democracy." We are still at an early point in this process, but some tentative conclusions can be made. In each central area—politics, government, and community building—there is now a sufficient track record to get a clearer sense of how well and to what ends information-based technologies are being used. Given the scale of the changes that are occurring, it is not surprising to discover that problems are being encountered. But IT has unmistakably moved from being something of a novelty to being part of the infrastructure supporting the daily activities of governments, citizens, and community organizations across the country.

The transactional efficiency and round-the-clock availability of information-based technologies ensure their expanded use. Driven in part by the demands of e-commerce, applications have become versatile and user-friendly. Not surprisingly, e-procurement was one area in which governments made early use of this technology.

Lowering barriers to adoption has accelerated the diffusion of IT into non-commercial areas as well. Although the rate of increase in Internet usage has slowed recently, it is clear that the volume and range of activities undertaken using IT will continue to grow. For example, a number of jurisdictions are now linking detailed geographic information system maps to databases of local government activities to pinpoint problems and improve the efficiency of service delivery. As technological capabilities increase and service and other costs decrease, governments and other users will make further application of these technologies.

One prospect being debated today holds particular importance for developing e-democracy. The interactive capability of connecting citizens with government officials through such means as real-time "netcasting"—of a committee meeting or conducting an online survey or opinion poll—prefigures the possibility of creating an institutional arrangement to foster direct rather than representative democracy. Given the existing structure of our political system, the degree to which such an arrangement could or should be created is unclear. However, the possibility points up one of the central underlying issues regarding e-democracy and the impact of IT on civic engagement. Information-based technologies can make certain outcomes more probable by reducing barriers or increasing efficiencies. But no decision about how to make use of new technologies occurs in a vacuum. There is always a political context that shapes development of the technology and influences the choice about how and to what ends the technology is used.

In other words, technology gives us choices, but we are the ones who must make them. The Internet can be merely a medium for private entertainment, but it can also become a means for public deliberation. Its existence does not increase political participation without people choosing to take advantage of its possibilities and become better informed and more engaged. Through this issue of the *National Civic Review* and this year's national conference on governance, the National Civic League hopes to encourage debate and reflection on how we want to use information-based technologies to advance democratic values and civic engagement.

CHRISTOPHER T. GATES
PRESIDENT, NATIONAL CIVIC LEAGUE

Civic Renewal and the Commons of Cyberspace

Peter Levine

This article brings together two current discussions. One—which is already familiar to readers of the *National Civic Review*—concerns the somewhat shaky condition of American civil society. The other investigates the Internet as a particular kind of public resource, a "commons." By bringing these discussions together, I hope to stimulate thinking about how the Internet might help to revitalize civil society. I also want to draw attention to developments that are threatening to spoil the Internet's civic potential.

People who are concerned about America's civil society believe that our habits and skills of association have weakened over time. Robert Putnam and others argue that joining associations and participating in loose cooperative networks (especially those that unite diverse people) makes the economy more efficient, introduces citizens to politics, increases the level of knowledge about public issues, helps to solve social problems without high financial cost or government coercion, and even promotes psychological and physical health.[1] Some people doubt Putnam's narrative portraying a decline in the health of civil society, arguing that he has romanticized the civil society of the 1950s and overlooked some contemporary strengths.[2] In my own view, the biggest problem is the deterioration of certain institutions that once helped ordinary people wield power while generating broad discussion of public issues, especially unions, political parties, civil rights organizations, and metropolitan daily newspapers.[3] I am not convinced that we have found substitutes for these institutions. But even if our civil society is reasonably strong compared to past decades, this is no reason for complacency. In each generation, it takes conscious effort to sustain old networks and associations and to bring new ones to life.

The second discussion, regarding the Internet as a commons, may be less familiar to readers of this journal. Some legal scholars and public-interest advocates (and computer hackers) view the Internet as a resource that is neither divided among separate property holders nor managed directly by the state. In a commons, volunteers donate labor to sustain a shared property, deliberate about its governance, and allow the whole community to reap its benefits.

As examples, consider forests and streams near a medieval manor, or a grassy area in the middle of an old New England town.[4] (I hope that we can note some attractive features of these historical examples without imagining that the Sheriff of Nottingham's England or Cotton Mather's Massachusetts was an ideal place to live.) Officially, the commons belonged to the crown or the state, but in practice the government was distant. Networks of local citizens actually managed the commons as if it were their shared property. Because they cut firewood, grazed cattle, and held fairs on the public land, they benefited as individuals working in a nascent market economy. But the land itself was not a commodity that anyone could buy or sell.

People must exhibit mutual trust, habits and skills of collaboration, and public spirit in order to sustain such a common resource against the tendency of individuals to abuse it. If their work succeeds, they may gain knowledge and inspiration that they can then transfer to other joint endeavors. In short, a successful commons relies on social capital—and generates more of it. A commons does not require or imply a *democracy* (think again of medieval Europe and puritan New England). But if its users are equal citizens with full civil rights living under a representative government, then their commons can be a powerful democratic resource. Indeed, Alexis de Tocqueville attributed the vitality of America's democracy to citizens' work in building free, local, public assets: "The Americans make associations to give entertainments, to found seminaries, to diffuse books, to build inns, to construct churches, to send missionaries to the antipodes; in this manner they found hospitals, prisons, and schools."[5]

The Commons of Cyberspace

Just a few years ago, the Internet seemed to be a rare modern example of a functioning commons. It is true that most of the software and equipment was manufactured by private companies and purchased by individuals or corporations. (The main exceptions were some popular free programs for sending e-mail and sharing files.) However, the overall system was structured by rules that had been devised collaboratively, that were open for public inspection, and that belonged to no one. These rules ensured that most types of privately manufactured hardware, software, and files were treated exactly alike. No company had intellectual property rights to crucial parts of the network. Anyone could turn text, sound, or images into strings of numbers and send them to any other Internet user, across all kinds of privately owned wires and machines, without worrying that the message would be appropriated, manipulated, or held up on its way. In the terminology used by Lawrence Lessig and others, the Internet had an "open architecture."[6]

Moreover, the mechanisms that routed Internet communications to their correct destinations were simple. What made the Internet a rich and exciting space were the programs—and the text, data, and images—that resided in people's desktop computers. Power was not centralized, as in a telephone network, but distributed among millions of diverse and largely autonomous users. As a result, groups of cooperating individuals could invent utterly unanticipated devices (such as the World Wide Web) to exploit the deliberately "stupid" underlying network.[7]

In those days, all Web pages and e-mail messages and many important programs were still "open source," meaning anyone could see how they had been constructed and imitate them. Users could enhance the models they found in cyberspace, so that the standard design of Web pages and discussion forums constantly improved.

People used the Internet not only to view others' material but also to build sites and disseminate free text and pictures, creating a gigantic commonwealth of public information. Usually, there is a reason not to contribute goods to a common pool: others may use them up without donating anything of equal value. But this problem is reduced if goods take a digital form, because they can be used many times over without harm. Of course, not all of these goods were unqualifiedly beneficial. The free material that was available online included not just genuine public *goods* but pirated pornography, false rumors, and racist screeds as well. But at least people had a rare opportunity to generate free and nondegradable common resources at low cost. Open architecture, free content, and norms of sharing together made a true commons in cyberspace.

Anecdotal evidence suggests that active participants in this commons sometimes formed intense social and civic bonds that transferred to the offline world. For instance, Howard Rheingold describes the profound friendships and networks of mutual support that developed because of the WELL, a San Francisco-based computer network that functioned as a commons.[8] We do not have enough statistical evidence to tell whether these anecdotes are typical. For one thing, surveys have not asked people whether they make their own Web pages, moderate online discussions, or write software, so we cannot assess the relationship between this kind of public work and civil society more generally. Even if it were the case that the people who helped build the cybercommons were heavily engaged in social and civic life, this would not prove that the Internet was responsible for their good citizenship. (Maybe they used the Internet because they were active citizens.) Thus there is insufficient evidence to prove that more widespread use of the cybercommons will revive American civil society. I think it will, because working together on shared, public projects is an excellent way to develop habits and skills of association.

Threats to the Cybercommons

Unfortunately, the electronic commons is under intense pressure today. In fact, some people detect a modern "enclosure movement" comparable to the takeover of English medieval commons by the seigneurial class.[9] Here I have space to mention just a few skirmishes in a larger conflict that has important civic implications.

First, the most valuable "real estate" on the Internet is scarce, and much of it is privately held. McDonald's wants its Web page to appear when you search for the word *hamburger*—but so do Burger King, People for the Ethical Treatment of Animals, and the City of Hamburg. Only ten or twenty Websites actually appear on the first page of results when you search for an important word or phrase. Since the owners of search engines are private companies, they may steer us to sites that belong to their own business partners. In any case, they use secret and proprietary methods to index only select portions of the World Wide Web. (Even the best ones cover no more than 16 percent of the whole.[10]) Meanwhile, just one entity can control any given domain name, and some names are more prominent than others. The owners of www.politics.com and www.freedom.org have claimed precious pieces of the commons.

Second, the valuable resources of the Internet are not like trees that grow on public land without human attention. It takes work and inspiration to build an exciting Web page that can draw an audience, but it also takes capital and marketable skills. Most people, and even most small organizations, cannot produce content that is worth looking at. Already, according to the Center for Digital Democracy, the top four "digital media properties (AOL Time Warner, Microsoft, Yahoo, and Lycos) . . . attract more visitors than the next 14 combined. And the top 10 companies (which include NBC, Disney, and Amazon) attract more visitors than the rest of the top 50 combined. The traffic patterns of today's web, in other words, are much closer to those of network television in the 1960s than to those of the Internet in the early 1990s."[11] This is a problem of civic significance, because it means the Internet is turning into a relatively passive medium rather than a commons sustained by the whole community of users.

Third, much of the Internet consists of completely proprietary space whose architecture is controlled by the owner. One such space is AOL's portal, through which millions of people go online. AOL makes the law within its own domain, structuring the whole experience of "the Internet" for its customers. For instance, the company has made sure that it can communicate en masse with all its customers, but its discussion groups are limited to twenty-six people. Therefore, customers cannot organize themselves against AOL.[12] An official from Microsoft complains that AOL "has erected a walled garden of captive users, and their strategy is to feed them Time Warner content." But AOL makes the same charge in return, predicting "consumers will use Microsoft software to view Microsoft content on Microsoft networks."[13] The emergence of two or three huge walled gardens does not mean the utter extinction of amateur Websites, independent discussion groups, and open networks. It does mean, though, that most of the audience, energy, and investment is taken out of the commons.

Fourth, most valuable software and even many corporate Web pages and e-mails are no longer open source. Technically, it is extremely difficult to see how sites and programs are constructed, and their design is covered by patents or copyrights that make imitation illegal. Even the "business methods" used by companies such as Amazon.com have been patented (in violation of longstanding legal principles).[14] Most of us no longer look at other people's files using free and open-source software such as FTP; instead, we browse the Web using patented corporate products, such as Microsoft Explorer, that have deliberate biases built into their design. People who want their Websites to be seen must make them compatible with such products.

Fifth, companies are starting to use cable television lines and the broadcast spectrum to transmit huge amounts of data per second, thereby allowing the World Wide Web to evolve from a library of text and images into an arena full of moving pictures and sound. Although the broadcast spectrum is public property, it has been allocated to a few large companies that also make products to which they want to steer mass audiences.[15] Even if the government blocks broadcasters and cable operators from discriminating in favor of their own content (a fairly unlikely prospect), the transformation to moving pictures still gives an enormous competitive advantage to Hollywood over the local kid with a Web page.

The broadcast spectrum can also connect small, mobile devices such as cellular telephones to the Internet. Such devices are much less powerful than computers, so the software they use must often be stored on a mainframe computer. Since the same companies that produce the mobile devices also own these computers, they are able to steer their customers to certain services and Web pages.[16]

Protecting Cyberspace as a Commons

These threats to the cybercommons should worry anyone who is concerned about civil society, social capital, and civic health. Most Americans will soon be connected to the thing called the Internet, but it may not be a commons built by millions of citizens. It may instead be a venue for news, information, and entertainment provided by professional employees of just a few companies. The majority of people will enter the Internet through some kind of portal (perhaps on their television screens or mobile phones) that nudges them toward corporate material. Although some of this material may be excellent, its purpose is to maximize profits, not to support civil society. Some citizens and small organizations will continue to create material of their own, but it will be increasingly difficult to find, because the owners of portals and proprietary networks have no incentive to highlight it.

If this happens, then there is no reason to predict an increase in social capital as a result of Internet use. On the contrary, we might expect most Americans to react like those Pittsburgh citizens who were given free Internet access (but little training) on the condition that they regularly logged onto the 'Net. They began to communicate less with other members of their own households, their social networks narrowed, and they reported a higher level of depression.[17] Likewise, the Stanford Institute for the Quantitative Study of Society gave thirty-five thousand people access to Microsoft's WebTV, a simple Internet connection. The new Internet users began spending less time with family and friends, attended fewer social events, and they devoted less time to the newspaper.[18] Both experiments essentially turned people into passive users of a rapidly commercializing Internet, and the civic results were discouraging.

We must strive to protect cyberspace as a commons; this means taking deliberate action on several levels. First, it is important to keep the architecture of the Internet open. The traditional medieval commons had to be physically accessible, lying near the village and not surrounded by impassible forests or private lands. Similarly, people must be able to find, receive, publish, and transmit just the data they want—even if they browse with Microsoft Explorer or connect to the Internet by way of a cell phone. Unless the federal government intervenes, companies that provide Internet access will surely discriminate in favor of their own content.

Second, the medieval commons was only worthwhile if stocked with fodder, tinder, spring water, and fish. Likewise, the cybercommons must feature valuable and exciting goods that are accessible to all. Producing such content in digital form may require subsidies by the government, or at least by large foundations. The *Digital Promise* report by Lawrence Grossman and Newton Minow recommends auctioning the broadcast spectrum and using the resulting revenues to fund nonprofit institutions that generate free online material.[19] I have some concerns about the governance structure that *Digital Promise* recommends, because it may unduly favor established institutions. But some kind of public support is probably essential.

Finally, the medieval commons required a network of individuals who knew how to work together and who valued their common property. Today, a broad group of stakeholders is developing the idea of a Public Telecommunications Service (PTS), whose main task will be to build such citizen networks in the digital age. Our assumption is that people will only value open architecture, public subsidies, and other features of a cybercommons if they personally use the Internet for public work. If they assume that the purpose of the Internet is to deliver entertainment quickly and cheaply, then they will not resist the privatization of public spaces.

Some local civic projects are quite inspiring. For example, since 1994 the Seattle Community Network (www.scn.org) has offered a single community portal leading to diverse Web pages. It provides free services such as an "education program which teaches computer and e-mail usage to those new to computers; a helpdesk and voicemail service for our user base; [and] hosting for small regional nonprofit organizations, including Web page mentoring." SCN enacts policies regarding civility, privacy, and other important civic issues only after public deliberation, thereby enhancing democratic participation and civic values. More recently, Hmong and Latino young people on the west side of St. Paul, Minnesota, have begun building the St. Paul Information Commons, a Website that maps the assets of their community and reflects their cultures.

However, most of the nonprofit, participatory, community-based Websites that sprang up in the 1990s have since closed. They were often poorly funded; they were difficult to find because search engines and private portals would not list them prominently; and they lost market share to commercial Websites in the same cities. Now that our eyes are open to the difficulty of operating in a commercial landscape, we must find ways to construct new community projects, to sustain them over time, and to connect them into larger networks. The future of the Internet as a commons depends on it—and American civil society itself may be at stake.

Notes

1. Putnam, R. D. *Bowling Alone: The Collapse and Revival of American Community.* New York: Simon & Schuster, 2000.

2. See for example Wills, G. "Putnam's America." *American Prospect,* July 12, 2000, pp. 34–37.

3. Levine, P. *The New Progressive Era: Toward a Fair and Deliberative Democracy.* Lanham, Md.: Rowman and Littlefield, 2000.

4. The classic theoretical treatment is Ostrom, E. *Governing the Commons: The Evolution of Institutions for Collective Action.* New York: Cambridge University Press, 1990. Ostrom describes "common pool resource" systems that are still extant in Switzerland, Spain, Japan, and the Philippines. Examples from medieval England or colonial America would be more difficult to analyze, but Ostrom suggests that these cases probably shared key features with their modern counterparts. See also Taylor, M. *The Possibility of Cooperation.* New York: Cambridge University Press, 1987.

5. De Tocqueville, A. *Democracy in America, Vol. II.* (H. Reeve and others, trans.) New York: Vintage, 1954, book two, chapter five, p. 114.

6. See for instance Lessig, L. "Innovation, Regulation, and the Internet." *American Prospect,* Mar. 27, 2000.

7. Reed, D. P., Saltzer, J. H., and Clark, D. D. "Comment on Active Networking and End-to-End Arguments." *IEEE Network,* 1998, *12* (3), 69–71.

8. Rheingold, H. *The Virtual Community: Homesteading on the Electronic Frontier.* (Rev. ed.) Cambridge, Mass.: MIT Press, 2000.

9. See for example Benkler, Y. "From Consumers to Users: Shifting the Deeper Structures of Regulation Toward Sustainable Commons and User Access." *Federal Communications Law Journal,* 2000, *52* (3), pp. 561–579.

10. Introna, L. D., and Nissenbaum, H. "Shaping the Web: Why the Politics of Search Engines Matters." *Information Society,* 2000, *16* (3), 1–17. For a public search engine and other proposals, see Chin, A. "Making the World Wide Web Safe for Democracy: A Medium-Specific First Amendment Analysis." *Hastings Communications and Entertainment Law Journal,* 1997, *19,* pp. 311–338.

11. E-mail from Jeffrey Chester of the Center for Digital Democracy, May 16, 2001.

12. Lessig, L. *Code and Other Laws of Cyberspace.* New York: Basic Books, 1999.

13. Klein, A. "For AOL and Microsoft, It's High-Tech Noon." *Washington Post,* June 8, 2001, p. A1.

14. Bollier, D. *Public Assets, Private Profits: Reclaiming the American Commons in an Age of Market Enclosure.* Washington, D.C.: New America Foundation, 2001.

15. Bollier (2001).

16. Hatfield, D. "A Look at the Promise and Policy Implications of New Wireless Technologies." Address at the Ford Foundation Digital Media Forum, Alexandria, Va., May 30, 2001.

17. Kraut, R., and others. "A Social Technology That Reduces Social Involvement and Psychological Well-Being?" *American Psychologist,* 1998, 53, 1017–1031.

18. Stanford Institute for the Quantitative Study of Society. "Internet Study." 2000. (www.stanford.edu/group/siqss/Press_Release/internetStudy.html)

19. See www.digitalpromise.org.

Peter Levine is a research scholar at the University of Maryland's Institute for Philosophy and Public Policy.

Access for All: Public Library Contributions to Civic Connectivity

Danielle Patrick Milam

The readiness factors for "wired" civic engagement are infrastructure, content, and training. American public libraries, particularly those in metropolitan areas, are helping communities build the infrastructure, organize and link content, and provide the training that result in a connected community. This article highlights the continuing role of the urban public library in promoting equitable access to information, linking citizens with local government and community services, and improving the competencies of all community residents in accessing, using, and creating virtual community resources.

Supported by a mix of private, public, and foundation funding, the urban public library is equipping its facilities downtown and in the neighborhoods with the technological tools that ensure public access to electronic information and the Internet. The development of this infrastructure is tied to new library buildings springing up in neighborhoods and downtowns across the country, sometimes in joint use with other community service providers and, increasingly, with intense community involvement.

Metropolitan libraries are supporting, alone and in collaboration, development of content on library Websites that organize and link people to a menu of current information resources on government, community and private sector agencies, and nonprofit organizations. The number of links to local, regional, and national information sources on library Websites is soaring. Content is being arranged to facilitate information seeking by diverse users.

The biggest challenge facing the community in this era of rapid technological change is to make technological tools available while ensuring and facilitating their use. Understanding the gap in competencies and comfort in the use of technology and electronic information, many urban public libraries are developing in-house or collaborative training with community partners for a range of audiences: children, teens, families, seniors, the underemployed and unemployed, small businesses, students, and lifelong learners. With the influx of new Americans to metropolitan areas, the public library is offering multilingual online sources and services that disseminate important civic information on the new American neighborhood and ties to the "home" community across the globe.

The ultimate impact of the urban public library in building community access to electronic information is revitalization of the library as a community place. Betty Jane Narver, executive board chair of the Urban Libraries Council, an association of 130 public libraries in major national metropolitan centers, says that "even as our public libraries are rapidly responding to the challenges of the new technology, they are becoming stronger community learning places. They have always been welcoming and generous places where people can find one-on-one help, whatever their information or learning needs might be. Today, libraries are the places where people can ask questions, receive help in finding answers, get training, and learn to feel comfortable in the use of technology and electronic information. Libraries, without abandoning their powerful traditional roles, are now using new tools to link people to the community resources that are available to them."

Building the Infrastructure for Access

Access for all is a traditional core value of the American public library. In the past, this has meant free, equitable and private access to sources of information inside the library, funded primarily with taxpayer revenues. Adding digital access has challenged the public library to continue its print collection development while investing in equipment and services that support new digital resources.

The urban public library has been an early community adopter of technology, first moving its internal functions and operations to automated, networked services; and acquiring public-access computers, software, and digitized collections. A study commissioned by the National Commission on Libraries and Information Science shows an overall increase in public library connectivity by more than 21 percent between 1998 and 2000. Massive deployment of public library Internet connectivity plans has resulted in 97.7 percent of urban public libraries and 97.3 percent of suburban libraries offering Internet access to the public.[1] The average number of public library public-access Internet terminals is 17.3 per site, with a range from 1 to 700. In suburban libraries, the average is 8.7 terminals, with a range of 1 to 220.

Libraries have received help in funding this digital infrastructure from a variety of public, private, and foundation sources. Federal funding has come from sources such as the E-rate program, which reimburses providers for above-cost services extended to high-cost urban and rural areas; the Telecommunications and Information Infrastructure Assistance Program (TIIAP), which has sponsored planning, demonstration, and access projects designed to ensure equal public access; and state block grant funding through the Library Services Construction Act and Library Services and Technology Act. State-level programs, such as the Texas Telecommunications Infrastructure Fund (TIF), have also been developed to help states and cities compete in the information economy.

Cities have adopted bond issues, launched sales tax initiatives, and tapped tax increment financing districts to develop "wired" communities. For example, in Memphis, Tennessee, a $100 million Information Hub initiative has been launched to improve the new central library with technology and digital information resources. In Chicago, the Neighborhoods Alive plan for improvements to sixty-three of its seventy-eight branch library facilities represents a deliberate strategy to "wire" neighborhoods through key public investments in buildings and technology. In Providence, Rhode Island, a $30 million initiative, Expanding Possibilities, includes support for operating programs that partner with schools, address the digital divide, and provide new-American and family literacy services, in addition to library facility improvement.[2]

Foundation investments have also greatly affected community access through investment in public library technology centers. For example, by the end of 2000, the Bill and Melinda Gates Foundation had already invested $83 million in its U.S. initiative to wire fifty-six hundred public libraries in low-income communities with more than twenty-five thousand computers. Many other national, regional, and local foundations are contributing to public library projects and programs that further public access to computers and the Internet.

The public library is also working with the private sector on infrastructure development. In Youngstown, Ohio, the library is working with the high-tech sector to build a high-speed network with a business incubator to foster growth of that sector in the region. Many of the corporate high-tech players in Seattle have been instrumental in helping the public library develop the technology plan for the new central library facility designed by Rem Koolhaus.

In addition to infrastructure development inside its buildings, the public library is developing innovative approaches to deploy mobile technology labs. Again in Memphis, the traditional bookmobile has been transformed into an "info bus," taking access to print and online materials in multiple languages to underresourced communities. The Multnomah County Library, serving the Portland, Oregon, area, has developed Cyber Seniors, a special outreach project created to teach senior citizens to use computers and, by bringing portable computers to senior citizen centers, offer peer instruction and guidance on learning to navigate and find Internet-based information.

The urban public library is an integral part of the community's infrastructure for connectivity. Additionally, it has gained important experience in operating community technology access sites, working with community partners such as schools and nonprofit organizations to serve a diverse and growing number of technology users. This experience and capacity is important for a community adapting to new forms of information and civic exchange.

Organizing Content for Virtual Community Connection

The library has always been the place where worlds reside—on paper. Today, it creates and organizes worldwide, Web-based information that promotes connection to local resources for civic information and engagement.

The library first began collecting and organizing community information during the urban unrest of the 1960s, arising from the desire to respond to community needs and foster collaboration among community service agencies. The focus was on linking community residents with local support resources.[3] Through the years, community information librarians have adopted new technologies, including database and geographic information systems, to design, organize, and deliver community information online.

The most recent inventory of best practices in community information sites is available at the University of Michigan's Website for the project "How Libraries and Librarians Help" (www.si.umich.edu/libhelp/best.htm).[4] The broad categories developed for the inventory demonstrate the breadth of organized content being developed and made available to the public on library Websites: "agency/local government content," "community information databases," "access issues/digital divide," digitized collections," "geographic information systems," "partnerships," "public library-community network initiatives," and "interactive community information or community network features."

Most urban public libraries have organized their Websites to connect users to broad categories of local and regional information within one to three mouse clicks. Moving toward ease of search and use, library sites are using multiple systems, including directories and search engines. For example, in Minnesota the Hennepin County Public Library's "eLibraries" connect users in one click on the home page to such link "centers" as FamilyLinks, LawLinks, KidLinks, SeniorLinks, WorldLinks, LearningLinks, and so forth. Within each center there are further directories and search functions.

Content for the public library Website is being developed locally to meet local information and learning needs. Although librarians and information technology staff are important resources for developing and maintaining sites, they are working closely with community, government, business, and information vendors to develop content. In Providence, the public library helps the city design and maintain the Child Opportunity Zone Information Network as part of a community effort to enhance awareness and use of community resources for families and youth. In Baltimore County, the public library is working with the County Department of Economic Development to offer demographic and business information online.

An important aspect of making Web-based community information easy to use is organizing for market segments. On the "Cleveland Links Library," you can search for Cleveland community information by subject under a variety of topics; each search can be further narrowed by clicking on "new sites" (recently added links) or "Sites Good4Kids." Responding to the borough's ever-changing immigrant constituency, the Queens Borough Public

Library, with support from AT&T, has developed WorldLinQ, a global portal that features journals, literature, and information in Chinese, French, Korean, Spanish, and Russian, and a directory of immigrant-serving agencies. The Seattle Public Library's catalogue of community information resources, available in English and Spanish, has been organized for teens and parents alike.

The urban public library's Website is introducing the community to complex technology tools in ways that relate to people's everyday activities. The Carnegie Library of Pittsburgh, whose operating budget supports the community information network Three Rivers Free-Net, offers regional nonprofit and government agencies the opportunity to share their stories by way of no-cost Websites. New nonprofit organization links, only one section of the Three Rivers Free Net, have expanded from 170 in 1997 to 1,295 today.

Similarly, the Enoch Pratt Free Library in Baltimore has a "Neighborhood Information Resources" section on its Web page, promoting community use of geographic-based information systems. The section allows access to metropolitan and neighborhood maps on demographic and environmental data and links users to neighborhood planning and mapping tutorials.

Web-based library information is increasing public access to and use of sources of community information that once required a great effort to gather and view. The Denver Public Library's collection of resources on the history of the American West, and Nashville's archives on the civil rights movement, are two examples where historical materials, including rare manuscripts, photographs, and personal letters, can now be accessed from both remote and library-based computers. The St. Louis Public Library's "Electronic City Hall" is organized for citizens who want to do business in the city, follow the progress of pending legislation, or research past legislation. The Seattle Public Library has a directory of online municipal codes from cities all over the country, so that citizens have an easy way to compare local codes with those in other municipalities.

Interactive Web features, leading the movement toward truly wired civic engagement, are also evident on library Websites. In Seattle, the library Website solicits community comments and recommendations on the new central facility. The Boston Public Library has launched a pilot interactive online tutor program with real-time teen homework help. This past year has seen an explosion in the number of public libraries deploying online, interactive, twenty-four/seven reference search services.

Training and Commitment to Human Development

Much of the discussion of community access to and adoption of technology is centered on the ease and importance of remote use. Many of the fears being expressed reflect the assumption that technology may result in increased social isolation and insufficient engagement in civic activities. Studies such as the Pew Internet and American Life Project are dispelling those fears, showing that Internet users engage in social activity just as frequently as nonusers. A survey for America Online and *American Demographics* indicates that social relationships are actually strengthened by online use.[5]

The experience of the public library in the digital age corroborates the evidence that technology strengthens social relationships. The urban public library is seeing a tremendous amount of use by new constituencies because of the new technology resources: seniors who come to use e-mail, teens who come to surf the 'Net and complete homework assignments, and small business owners who come to use expensive finance and business planning databases.

The latest National Telecommunications and Information Administration study reports that the digital inclusion rate is rapidly increasing in the United States, with more than half of all households having computers.[6] It also counts fifty-one million people who used the Internet only outside the home. Of those, 1.9 percent report having access only through the public library. Certain groups, such as African Americans (2.9 percent), Asian and Pacific Islanders (2.3 percent) and the unemployed (4.3 percent), are more likely to use the public library for access.

For an urban public library serving a low-income population, the digital divide is not a concept but a reality; the new users often represent the demographics of technology have-nots. For example, at Teen'scape, a technology center at the Los Angeles Public Library's downtown location, a large part of everyday users are young minority males. Libraries have gained important insights on how to attract new users. An important reason the Teen Central cybercenter in Phoenix is so popular for this same user group is that, in the design and build-out, the library and its architect involved city teens intensively. From drawing "dream" centers to picking out furniture and fabrics, teens helped plan and celebrate the birth of their special place.

The deep understanding that a public library gains in developing the technology competencies and comfort of its own staff aids its understanding of and ability to have an impact on technology use in and by the communities it serves. A quick survey of urban public library Websites points to an array of training programs available to serve the learning needs of both the general public and special populations. Many libraries are staffing up and creating technology training centers in addition to public-access cybercenters to handle the increasing demand for training.

These computer training programs reflect the needs of local users. For example, the Broward County (Florida) Public Library's "information gateway" training menu is targeted at the growing number of Hispanics and seniors in the community. Computer classes are offered, in English, and Spanish, on basic computer literacy, creating a Website, e-mail, finding genealogy information, government and health information, online auctions, investment and job information, news and current events, software programs, and writing rèsumès. In partnership with federal, state, and local service providers, many urban public libraries have developed a number of specialized training and literacy services for workforce agency clientele and adult learners having English as a second language. In St. Paul, Minnesota, and elsewhere, traditional library services such as story time are scheduled to coincide with job search counseling and support for parents.

The Get Smart—Get Connected project at the Brooklyn Public Library, using more than 850 public-access computers, holds free computer and Internet training for people of all ages. Among the regularly offered programs are Homework Help; Internet for Families; Education and Job Information; Introduction to the World Wide Web for Adults, Teens, and Children; and online research. This project is proving effective in reaching minorities, families with children, teens, single-parent households, and those of low economic means who are not able to invest in a home computer. It is also proving important in stimulating community collaboration and enhancing links between community information and service providers and community residents.

In these ways, the infusion of technology-based products and services has enhanced the library's role as a safe place and neutral ground. The directors of the new teen spaces in Los Angeles and Phoenix report that not only are record numbers of inner-city youths coming to their new exciting spaces but these young people are sharing computers, honoring the rules, and expressing appreciation for the resources. Virtually none of the initial fears (gang-related activities, inappropriate use of Internet search) have been realized. Instead, libraries are giving teens a new safe place to meet, and new ways to develop their voices. A number of public library–supported teen Websites with teen-produced content are appearing. Teen technology tutors are becoming a highly effective means of providing effective training to teen computer users. Indeed, there may be an institutional revolution in the making because of the impact of technology. At the Free Library of Philadelphia, youths employed as teen tech assistants have now lobbied successfully to change their job description to teen leadership assistant, reflecting the growing responsibilities they are assuming and the growing status of their jobs in the library.

Getting There: The Connected Community

The urban public library experience demonstrates how a community builds connection in the digital age while maintaining its important traditional role as a free, accessible, safe community place. The development of infrastructure, community information, and training is bringing community service providers and libraries together, as well as stimulating this important civic institution to reach out to the community and connect with citizens in powerful new ways. Libraries understand how to prepare and sustain virtual civic engagement as a critical part of community development. With their wealth of experience, public libraries have important lessons to share with their communities and their partners.

Notes

1. Bertot, J. C., and McClure, C. R. "Public Libraries and the Internet 2000: Summary Findings and Data Tables." Washington, D.C.: National Commission on Libraries and Information Science, Sept. 7, 2000.

2. Urban Libraries Council. "Public Library Contributions to Urban Economic Development." Evanston, Ill.: Urban Libraries Council, Mar. 2001.

3. Durrance, J. C., and Schneider, K. G. *Public Library Community Information Activities: Precursors of Community Networking Partnerships.* Ann Arbor: School of Information, University of Michigan, 1996.

4. Durrance, J. C., and Pettigrew, K. E. "Digital Community Services in Public Libraries." Project of School of Information, University of Michigan, and Information School, University of Washington. Funded by Institute of Museum and Library Services Washington, D.C. 2001. (www.si.umich.edu/libhelp/best.htm)

5. Weiss, M. J. "Online America." *American Demographics,* 2001, 23 (3), 53–57.

6. National Telecommunications and Information Administration. "Falling Through the Net: Toward Digital Inclusion." Washington, D.C.: National Telecommunications and Information Administration, Oct. 2000, pp. 1–4.

Danielle Patrick Milam is vice president for programs and development of the Urban Libraries Council in Evanston, Illinois. The views presented here are her personal statements and do not necessarily reflect the views of her employer.

If E-Democracy Is the Answer, What's the Question?

John D. Nugent

We've learned over the past year or so that certain fundamental economic axioms—primarily, the need for profitability and a sound business model—are not suspended in cyberspace, as an increasing number of dot com companies have found themselves looking unattractive to investors and customers. Ongoing development of "electronic democracy" and "e-government" raises a similar issue: Are political science axioms suspended in cyberspace? Given what we know about traditional forms of political participation and political representation (and the level of political knowledge) in the United States, should we expect the Internet to begin to alter those practices? Will it yield a higher level of participation by a better-informed citizenry? Will it bring more responsive and accountable elected officials and public bureaucracies, for example, or essentially replicate and reinforce them?

Since the American public's participation in most traditional forms of political activity has been modest, is there any reason to expect that public participation in newer, online forms of political activity will be any greater? Will our local, state, and federal political institutions—which are generally not designed to accommodate plebiscitary democracy—become more accountable and responsive if Americans use the Internet for political purposes? Indeed, are these even the right questions to be asking about how the Internet may affect American politics?

From the earliest days of the Internet, observers have speculated about the extent to which it would change how people interact with one another and with their elected officials. Predictions have ranged from the wildly optimistic to the darkly pessimistic. Howard Rheingold, one of the earliest analysts of online community building, noted in the early 1990s that "virtual communities could help citizens revitalize democracy, or they could be luring us into an attractively packaged substitute for democratic discourse."[1]

This article assesses the contributions the Internet is currently making to American politics at the federal, state, and local levels. As the title implies, assessing the political importance of the Internet depends a lot on the questions asked. I think the important ones we should be asking about e-government and e-democracy are not new but rather the same sort of questions political scientists and others have long been asking about American politics: What kind of citizen participation is necessary for a healthy democracy? How much do citizens need to know to vote wisely and hold their representatives accountable? Should our representatives exercise judgment, or simply reflect the wishes of their constituents? What should we expect from our local, state, and national governments?

The implications of the Internet for American democracy are not something to be determined in some utopian future; they are being seen now as citizens and governments apply information technology to the traditional things they have been doing all along. Although scholars have written a great deal about the philosophical implications of online communication for our understanding of human identity,[2] the immediate importance of the Internet for American democracy and governance revolves around four activities: (1) accessing political information online, (2) communicating about politics and government with other citizens and groups, (3) communicating with elected representatives and government officials, and (4) delivering government services online. Examples of each of these are discussed here.

What Sort of Democracy Do We Have in This Country?

For all its importance, the Internet has not remade the American political landscape. Like other communications media, it has supplemented the world in which it was created, and its political implications must be considered within the context of that world. As one scholar has noted, "every new electronic media technology this century, from film, AM radio, shortwave radio, and facsimile broadcasting to FM radio, terrestrial television broadcasting, cable TV, and satellite broadcasting, has spawned similar utopian notions. In each case, to varying degrees, visionaries have told us how these new magical technologies would crush the existing monopolies over media, culture, and knowledge and open the way for a more egalitarian and just society."[3]

A major reason technology has not lived up to such bold predictions is that political participation and governmental process are structured by institutions and processes established by state and federal constitutions, which are quite resistant to change. No new way of staying informed about current political events and communicating with elected officials changes the fact that laws are written by committee, debated and passed by legislature, carried out by executive-branch agency, and adjudicated in court. Political participation is important at each stage, but the system rewards long-term, diligent attention to often tedious and arcane processes much more than sporadic involvement, even if well-timed and well-informed. Americans in general have long gotten a mixed message concerning the value of their political participation. The American political system "celebrates the individual while longing for a sense of community. It allows almost unlimited participation while doing little to facilitate it. It combines thick civic responsibilities with thin civic identities. It has emerged as the world's leading democracy, but it is designed to limit the impact of the vox populi. And, perhaps most fundamentally, it is built upon both an abiding faith in and deep-seated suspicion of the public."[4] Put simply, a new technology or communications medium is more likely to reflect and supplement the existing political order than alter it.

The level of political participation in the United States has been generally quite modest in recent decades. According to the Federal Election Commission, voter turnout for presidential elections has been holding steady between approximately 50 and 55 percent of the voting-aged population since 1972, with a much lower rate of turnout for off-year congressional elections.[5] Obviously, voting is only one form of citizen participation; others include informing oneself about political candidates and issues, talking about politics with other people, attending political meetings or rallies, and donating time or money to a political candidate.

Survey data on this sort of political behavior have been systematically collected since the early 1950s, and on the whole the data, though crude, indicate consistently low levels of citizen interest and participation in politics. Over the last four decades, the University of Michigan's biennial National Election Study (NES) has asked Americans about their level of knowledge of and interest in politics, and the type of political activity they engage in.[6]

From 1964 to 1998, 25–42 percent of survey respondents indicated that they follow what's going on in government and public affairs "only now and then" or "hardly at all." In presidential election years between 1952 and 1996, between 17 and 31 percent reported they were "not much interested" in the campaign. A caveat to this sort of data is the level of interest in political campaigns as the source of jokes or as a form of entertainment. During the 2000 presidential campaign, a survey by the Pew Research Center for the People and the Press "showed that a full 47 percent of Americans between the ages of 18 and 29 often gleaned information about the presidential campaign from late-night comedy shows."[7]

From 1952 to 1998, 15–37 percent of NES survey respondents indicated that they had tried to influence how others vote. From 1956 to 1998, 5–21 percent of respondents said they had worn a campaign button or put a campaign bumper sticker on their car. From 1952 to 1998, 4–16 percent of respondents said they had donated money to a political campaign. During the same period, between 5 and 9 percent said they had attended a political meeting or rally, and 2 to 7 percent said they had worked for a political party or a candidate.

On the whole, then, Americans' level of interest in politics as well as their actual political participation have been modest. Scholars and journalists have hotly debated whether low interest and participation, coupled with declining trust in the federal government, constitutes a crisis of democracy in this country.[8] My purpose in citing these data is mainly to offer a rough baseline of the extent to which Americans pay attention to and participate in politics. If one hopes or believes that the Internet will lead otherwise uninterested and inactive Americans to learn about and participate in politics, it seems clear that there is plenty of room for improvement in this regard.

What Are the Primary Political and Governmental Uses of the Internet?

The Internet is obviously used for an array of purposes. It is a somewhat arbitrary exercise to separate those purposes with political implications from those without, since today's cultural or social issue may be the focus of tomorrow's legislation. As commonly used, *e-democracy* refers to processes carried out online—communicating with fellow citizens and elected representatives about politics, for example. *E-government* refers to the online version of bricks-and-mortar governmental institutions such as a state legislature, a driver's license bureau, or another agency delivering government services.

Most of the processes and institutions in cyberspace have an offline counterpart; there is little that is genuinely new about the online institutions and processes discussed here. A computer with an Internet connection and other peripherals can be viewed as a fast and reasonably cheap electronic version of several traditional technologies: the printing press, the archive, the telephone, the fax machine, the radio transmitter, the television studio. But the online version of these media can be used to gather, store, transmit, access, or communicate huge amounts of political information quickly and over a great distance, and these features hold important consequences for politics.

According to the Nielsen polling organization, about 170 million American households (60 percent) have access to the Internet.[9] This number seems to be holding relatively steady after several years of a consistent increase in the number of Americans online.[10] A November 2000 poll commissioned by the Democracy Online Project gives some sense of how the Internet affected people's political thought and behavior during the 2000 campaign cycle.[11] Fifty-five percent of the survey's respondents reported that they use the Internet. Of these users, 35 percent reported using the Internet to get information about politics, campaigns, or issues in the news. (Interestingly, these figures are much higher than those in Britain during the 2001 parliamentary elections, in which "only a tiny minority of voters . . . used the internet for election information, despite massive investment by all the main parties in their online presence and a rising tide of hyperbole about the democratic potential of the web."[12]) Thirty-nine percent of American Internet users reported sending or receiving e-mail about the election with friends or family; 25 percent were contacted by or got information about political campaigns; 10 percent contacted partisan interest groups over the Internet; 10 percent participated in a live chat or Web-based discussion forum; 2 percent contributed money to nonpartisan organizations; and 1 percent donated money to a political candidate.

As I have noted, many Americans view politics as a source of entertainment or material for jokes. Consistent with this notion is the finding by the Democracy Online poll that 54 percent of respondents sent or received e-mail jokes about the candidates or the campaign, a figure that presumably reflects the events of the thirty-six-day postelection Florida recount and litigation period. Such figures raise questions about the quality of the "political" content of Americans' online newsgathering. If political figures and events are treated as entertainment rather than an important element of citizenship, then the impact of the Internet on American politics may be limited.

Accessing Political Information Online. At the most basic level of gathering political (and other) information, the world's news is readily available to anyone with access to the World Wide Web. Nearly all newspapers and television stations have Websites that mirror or supplement their traditional coverage, and many people get headline news when logging onto Web portals such as Yahoo! (www.yahoo.com) to check their e-mail or search the Web. It seems likely that well-informed individuals use such news sources to broaden their news intake, while politically uninterested or poorly informed Internet users ignore online political news just as they would otherwise. It is true that the Internet and other information technologies "help decentralize access to information—about political and legal processes, about policy critiques, and about resistance strategies and organization,"[13] but these benefits are only as good as the user's ability to locate and use a variety of independent and eclectic news outlets. Individuals with little interest in politics are likely to rely on the same sort of news they would use offline.

It is clear that the consolidation of traditional media outlets into fewer and fewer hands[14] is being reproduced online as well. A June 2001 report by Jupiter Media Metrix, a firm that measures use of the Internet and new technologies, found that "the total number of companies controlling 50 percent of US user minutes online shrank 64 percent, from 11 to four, between March 1999 and March 2001. Even more drastic was the drop in the number of companies controlling 60 percent of all US minutes spent online: from 110 in March 1999 to 14 in March 2001, an 87 percent decrease."[15] Refuting the notion that market dominance is impossible on the Internet, the report concludes that "the Internet may provide an opportunity for new players such as Microsoft or Yahoo! to become serious media companies, but so far a major share of the market is being absorbed by a handful of companies, with those same companies continuing to direct traffic across their own networks of sites." As an increasing number of Americans access the Internet through cable television rather than the phone line, they are subject to restrictions and fees imposed by a handful of cable giants.

A much-heralded feature of the Internet is its capacity to make available primary information that individuals can read and assess for themselves, without filtering or mediation by reporters or commentators. Most government institutions at the federal, state, and local levels have at least a basic Web presence.

Local and county governments have been the slowest to get online, but a survey of cities and counties cosponsored by the International City/County Management Association along with Public Technology, Inc., found that 93 percent of the responding jurisdictions had a Website or planned to have one within the next twelve months (that is, by autumn 2001).[16] The sites of federal agencies can all be accessed through the gateway site FirstGov (www.firstgov.gov), and state government home pages can be found by inserting a state's two-letter postal abbreviation into the address www.state.__.us. Pennsylvania has gone so far as to put its web address (www.state.pa.us) on its license plates to promote its e-government effort.

Governmental sites may provide information about governmental institutions, processes, and officeholders and thereby improve citizen understanding of government. The White House Website (www.whitehouse.gov), for example, offers continuously updated press releases concerning the president's activities and links to executive branch agency sites. In addition to this sort of basic information, the White House Website reveals general clues about how high a priority a president places on electronic government and provision of online information. For example, a scholar who monitored the first "Web transition"—between the Clinton and Bush administrations—at 12:01 p.m. on January 20, 2001, noted that the Bush administration was slow to get its site up and running after the Clinton administration site was taken down.[17]

In addition to the Websites of congressional committees and individual members of the House (www.house.gov) and Senate (www.senate.gov), the *Congressional Record* and the full text of bills considered and passed by Congress have been available at Thomas, the Library of Congress's Website (http://thomas.loc.gov), since January 1995. Since spring 2000, the U.S. Supreme Court has been online (www.supremecourtus.gov), although its opinions were previously available elsewhere online. The various branches of the federal government maintain high-quality Websites for its institutions and officials, and the vast scope of the federal government's use of communication and information technologies is indicated well by the publication *Federal Computer Week* (www.fcw.com). In an effort to further streamline and extend the federal government's efforts, a bill entitled the E-Government Act was introduced in the U.S. Senate in May 2001 to broaden and improve federal efforts. Specifically, the bill is intended (1) to bring effective leadership to federal government efforts to develop and promote electronic government services and processes by establishing the post of federal chief information officer within the Office of Management and Budget; (2) to establish measures that require using Internet-based information technology to enhance citizen access to government information and services, improve government efficiency and reduce government operating costs, and increase the opportunity for citizen participation in government; (3) to promote interagency collaboration in providing electronic government services, where this collaboration would improve the service to citizens by integrating related functions; and (4) to promote interagency collaboration in using internal electronic government processes, where this collaboration would improve the efficiency and effectiveness of the processes.

Communicating About Politics and Government with Other Citizens and Groups. Individuals can read and post to online bulletin boards and discussion lists, with one another or government officials. Web-based examples include the WELL (www.well.com), Salon's "Table Talk" (http://tabletalk. salon.com/webx?), Slate's "The Fray" (http://slate.msn.com/code/theFray/theFray.asp), the *New York Times* "forums" (http://forums.nytimes.com/comment/), the *Washington Post's* "Live Online" (http://washingtonpost.com/wp-srv/liveonline/schedule.htm), Plastic (www.plastic.com), Quorum (www. quorum.org), Debate America (www. debateamerica.org), and Free Republic's "Forum" (www.FreeRepublic.com/perl/ topics). Innumerable other discussion lists take the form of e-mail sent to list members (listservs). At its best, such discussion educates readers and encourages them to think about and join the debate over political issues and current events. At its worst, such "discussion" consists of hyperpartisan, unreflective, and superficial exchange about events of the day. As law professor Cass Sunstein argues in his book *Republic.com,* it may also allow participants to insulate themselves from viewpoints with which they disagree, which discourages free and open discussion of competing ideas.[18] Lists may be "moderated" by someone who performs a "gatekeeping" function, which may improve the quality of the discussion, although it may also result in unwarranted censorship of some individuals' comments.

At best, online discussion of this kind may generate interesting and thoughtful insight. Some lists, such as Slate, excerpt the most valuable comments ("Best of the Fray") to save readers the trouble of sorting through the chaff. Although it is difficult to measure how widespread the practice is, newspaper writers often include comments made in Internet chat rooms in their news stories,[19] indicating either that these are viewed as sources of informed opinion or that they have a novelty factor that may be short-lived.

In addition to government agencies and elected representatives, interest groups (and many other organizations) have been quick to go online to get their message out and recruit new members. Groups and voluntary associations have long been viewed as important to a thriving democracy, and they have received a great deal of scholarly and journalistic attention over the last ten years, building in part on Harvard political scientist Robert Putnam's work on "social capital"—the benefits (trust, reciprocity, information, cooperation) that a society gains from the civic engagement of its citizens. Putnam noted that citizen involvement in voluntary associations—clubs, churches, PTAs, sports leagues, and so forth—has declined substantially in the post–World War II era; he argues that this has important negative consequences for developing and maintaining social capital, which is critical for healthy communities and citizen satisfaction with their governments.[20]

Scholars continue to debate whether online interaction among citizens can build social capital, but it would seem that traditional face-to-face encounters with fellow citizens build stronger ties and permit easier consensus building and collective decision making. Howard Rheingold concludes that communications technologies can be important in facilitating contact among people, but that ultimately "most of what needs to be done has to be done face to face, person to person—civic engagement means dealing with your neighbors in the world where your body lives."[21] Thus, although it is certainly not a bad thing that the Internet provides Americans with a new way to talk about politics, these discussions seem unlikely to build as much social capital as traditional forms of citizen interaction.

Communicating with Elected Representatives and Government Officials. Electronic mail and other forms of Web-based communication hold promise as means of political communication between citizens and government officials. All members of Congress have e-mail addresses, so in theory it should be easy for citizens to communicate with their representatives. The bad news is that, according to a May 2001 report by the Congress Online Project of the Congressional Management Foundation and George Washington University, members of Congress received approximately eighty million e-mails in 2000—and the number is rising by a million per month.[22] E-mail is easy to send, and a message can be sent to every member of Congress almost as easily as to just one or two. As a result, "growing numbers of citizens are frustrated by what they perceive to be Congress' lack of responsiveness to e-mail. At the same time, Congress is frustrated by what it perceives to be e-citizens' lack of understanding of how Congress works and the constraints under which it must operate."[23] Thus the very ease of this form of communication is limiting its effectiveness; paradoxically, writing a letter by hand and mailing it the old-fashioned way may be the quickest and best way to get your representative's attention.

An individual can sign up to have daily or periodic e-mail updates from government agencies delivered directly to the desktop, such as the U.S. Department of Health and Human Services press release listserv (http://list.nih.gov/cgi-bin/wa?SUBED1=hhspress&A=1) and the various listservs maintained by the Department of Energy (www.energy.gov/subscriptions/index.html). Such services are obviously targeted at niche audiences, but they essentially eliminate for the recipient the cost of receiving government information.

Electronic petitions are also popular as a relatively easy way to send a message to an elected official. Such a petition may be initiated and circulated by individuals (who ask that you add your name and forward it to others) or initiated by such Web-based organizations as E the People (www.e-thepeople.com), Online Petition (www.petitiononline.com/), and Speak Out (www.speakout.com/petitions/). Like e-mail, however, these petitions seem to add to the overload of electronic communications being directed at lawmakers and probably contribute more to the signer's sense of self-satisfaction than to meaningful exchange between elector and elected.

The Online Delivery of Government Services. At the state and local levels in particular, it is increasingly possible to complete various governmental transactions online: paying a parking ticket or utility bill, making child support payments, registering to vote, bidding on a state contract, renewing a driver's license, obtaining a hunting or fishing license, applying for a government job, reporting needed streetlight repairs, or allowing parents to check the academic performance of a school. Maryland has passed legislation requiring that 80 percent of its services be moved online by 2004.[24] In his 2001 State of the State Address, Iowa Governor Tom Vilsack called for 100 percent of state government services to be online by 2003. In March 2000, the Arizona Democratic Party held its presidential primary online, the first instance of a legally binding online political election in this country. Many elected officials feel that moving delivery of government services online improves the responsiveness of government to citizens and thereby increases the level of confidence in those governments.

Has the Internet Enhanced American Democracy and Governance? The Internet activity with the most important implications for American politics is generally the online version of a traditional, offline form of political participation, albeit occurring much faster and more accessibly. There is clearly a great deal going on online that could alter how Americans learn about and participate in their governments, but as noted at the outset, it is also easy to overestimate the actual significance of these activities.

The Bad News. As noted above, Americans receive mixed messages about the necessity of participating in government. At the federal level in particular, many opportunities for individual participation exist, but few are really encouraged. Neither major political party seems to be in a hurry to increase voter turnout[25]; forming or joining an interest group or PAC has become the best way to influence federal policy making.[26] At the state and local levels, institutions are more open and accessible, although the public tends to pay much less attention to state and local politics than to national politics. One reason for this is that Washington, D.C., offers "one-stop shopping" for the politically interested and involved. If Congress passes a law, it is the law of the land, supplanting the rules and legislation of states and localities. The risk of failure is high, but the reward is commensurately great as well.

The traditional media coverage that most people tend to consume doesn't do much to sort out or explain the complexity of government at the local, state, and national levels. As Stephen Hess of the Brookings Institution notes, "for most Americans, whose news comes from local and network television, less often from local newspapers, it is news that pays little attention to municipal government other than the fire and police departments, that turns its back on state government, and that increasingly finds the margins of national government more interesting than the core."[27] A lot of this news coverage is simply reproduced online, which implies that increasing political knowledge is not necessarily the result of simply removing the barriers to accessing a wealth of information by logging on to the 'Net.

To know government is not necessarily to love government. Citizen trust in all levels of government has fallen dramatically over the past three decades; the reason for this is not merely related to ignorance about political issues or how governments work. Indeed, although Congress is the branch of the federal government most transparent and closest to the people, it is the branch that Americans say they like the least.[28] Increasing the amount of information people receive about Congress is likely to reduce public trust even further by exposing the arguing and compromising that is inherent to deliberation and the legislative process but that citizens find distasteful. Moreover, although citizens currently look with greater favor upon the executive branch and the U.S. Supreme Court, this attitude reflects the fact that the deliberations of these institutions are less visible to the public. As such, greater coverage of their inner workings would not necessarily improve the level of citizen trust in government.

The Good News. Once we apply a healthy discount rate to optimistic expectations for the Internet, there is something important to be said about how information technology can enhance how people learn about and participate in government. The Internet's contribution to the political process may be to make faster, easier, and less geographically constrained traditional forms of participation, but the added speed, ease, and spatially unfettered ability to transmit information may have important consequences during the legislative process, an election, a crisis, or a protest rally. During the commotion following Senator James Jeffords's May 2001 departure from the Republican Party, Steven Clift pointed out in an e-mail to the Democracies Online listserv that, "like the week after [the] Florida [recount], people turn to the Internet when there is a scarcity of information. This is an 'Internet moment.'" The political importance of the Internet may be seen periodically rather than continuously. Websites and e-mail have proven important in coordinating and publicizing the protests held around the world by the antiglobalization movement in a way that would have been impossible with traditional communications media.[29]

Although a great deal of the news coverage of political events does not inspire much confidence, there have always been high-quality newspapers and television and radio programming. For the politically interested individual, Internet access eliminates the barriers to obtaining the highest-quality political coverage and commentary, as well as the barriers to obtaining primary-source information about governmental agencies and institutions. It is too much to expect that the average American will suddenly seek out and consume such information, but the ways that politically attentive individuals—voters, activists, policy makers, educators, journalists, and others—experience politics and government are greatly enriched by online resources.

Ongoing efforts to provide government services online will likely have a positive effect on levels of citizen trust and confidence in their governments. Some research has indicated that citizen attitudes toward state and federal governments are shaped by ideology rather than the performance of those governments[30]; still, the survey data used in these studies don't allow us to conclude that citizen attitudes toward government would not be improved by having more user-friendly online government services such as those mentioned above. Given that many people's least favorite task is anything on the order of standing in line to renew a driver's license, it seems reasonable to believe that governments at all levels (as well as private-sector hardware and software vendors) are justified in their efforts to expand the scope of e-government.

Compared to other information technologies, the Internet is still in its infancy. Although an array of political and governmental activities now occur online, it is ultimately too early to predict how Americans will use the Internet for political purposes in, say, twenty years, once its novelty has completely worn off and the computer becomes no less common in households than the telephone or television.[31] No communications medium is well suited for every purpose. Just because we can access the World Wide Web on a cell phone doesn't mean that many people will do so. As the novelty of the Internet wears off and people settle into the pattern of usage that makes the most sense for their needs and interests, we will get a better sense of whether online political discussion groups, electronic petitions, and online voting stand the test of time and become a routine part of our political landscape.

Unlike the Internet, American political institutions are not built for speed. The deliberative process of a legislative body is not intended to be efficient; indeed, it would suffer from being made so. The executive branch of government is supposed to act with greater speed and efficiency, although we know that this is often not the case. There is probably no single accepted definition of what a "healthy democracy" or "responsive government" should look like, but it is clear that the Internet can facilitate a variety of activities that accord with most people's conception of the terms. Among the most important elements of a healthy democracy are reasonable expectations about what impact the citizen can expect to have on governmental process and institutions and what impact government can be expected to have on society. The Internet factors into each set of expectations by connecting people with one another and with their governments, and by facilitating delivery of governmental services online. The laws of politics are not suspended in cyberspace, but this does not mean that the Internet's implications for the political system are minor. Rather, the many elements of e-democracy (and e-government) are part of a much larger answer to these questions regarding what we ought to expect from our political processes and institutions.

Notes

1. Rheingold, H. *The Virtual Community: Homesteading on the Electronic Frontier.* Cambridge, Mass.: MIT Press, 2000, p. 295.

2. See, for example, Turkle, S. *Life on the Screen: Identity in the Age of the Internet.* New York: Touchstone, 1997.

3. McChesney, R. W. *Rich Media, Poor Democracy: Communications Politics in Dubious Times.* Urbana: University of Illinois Press, 1999, pp. 119–120.

4. Delli Carpini, M. X., and Keeter, S. *What Americans Know About Politics and Why It Matters.* New Haven: Yale University Press, 1996. p. 268.

5. See Federal Election Commission. http://www.fec.gov/pages/htmlto5.htm.

6. The complete data are available at www.umich.edu/~nes/nesguide/nesguide.htm.

7. Sella, M. "The Stiff Guy vs. the Dumb Guy." *New York Times Magazine,* Sept. 24, 2000, p. 74.

8. See, for example, Nye, J. S., Jr., Zelikow, P. D., and King, D. C. (eds.). *Why People Don't Trust Government.* Cambridge: Harvard University Press, 1996; Hibbing, J. R., and Theiss-Morse, E. (eds.). *What Is It About Government That Americans Dislike?* New York: Cambridge University Press, 2001; and Delli Carpini and Keeter (1996).

9. For the current figures, see http://209.249.142.27/nnpm/owa/NRpublicreports.usageweekly.

10. Stoughton, S. "Net Loss: As Novelty Wears Off, Time Spent Surfing Web Declines." Boston Globe, Apr. 8, 2001, p. A1.

11. See "Post-Election 2000 Survey on Internet Use for Civics and Politics," Dec. 4, 2000. http://democracyonline.org/databank/dec2000survey.shtml.

12. Millar, S. "First Internet-Era Election Proves Flop with Voters." *Guardian,* June 1, 2001. www.guardian.co.uk/guardianpolitics/story/0,3605,499434,00.html.

13. Smith, J. "Cyber Subversion in the Information Economy." *Dissent,* Spring 2001, p. 49.

14. Bagdikian, B. H. *The Media Monopoly.* (6th ed.) New York: Beacon Press, 2000.

15. "Rapid Media Consolidation Dramatically Narrows Number of Companies Controlling Time Spent Online, Reports Jupiter Media Metrix." (Press release.) June 4, 2001. www.jup.com/company/pressrelease.jsp?doc=pr010604. See also Kessler, M. "Net Arena Shrinks As Players Consolidate: Consumers Saddled with Fewer Choices, Higher Access Prices." *USA Today,* June 5, 2001, p. 1B.

16. "Is Your Local Government Plugged In? Highlights of the PTI/ICMA Electronic Government Survey." www.pti.org/docs/E-Gov2000.pdf.

17. See, for example, Lule, J. "Click and Learn at the White House Web Site." *Chronicle of Higher Education,* May 18, 2001, p. B13.

18. Sunstein, C. *Republic.com.* Princeton: Princeton University Press, 2001.

19. See, for example, Emerson, B. "Conversation and Conjecture: Conspiracy Theories Crowd Net, Burn Up Radio Talk Show Lines." *Atlanta Journal and Constitution,* Nov. 9, 2000, p. 2D; Schorow, S. "Wakefield Massacre; Chat Room Denizens Weigh In with Opinions on McDermott." *Boston Herald,* Dec. 28, 2000, p. 18; Kane, E. "Chmura Case Has Chat Rooms on Internet Buzzing." *Milwaukee Journal Sentinel,* June 1, 2000, p. 1B.

20. Putnam, R. D. *Bowling Alone: The Collapse and Revival of American Community.* New York: Simon & Schuster, 2000.

21. Rheingold (2000), p. 382.

22. Congress Online Project. "E-Mail Overload in Congress: Managing a Communications Crisis." www.congressonlineproject.org/email.html, posted Mar. 19, 2001.

23. Congress Online Project (2001).

24. Harris, S. "Tooting Your E-Horn." *Governing,* 2000, *13* (12), 48.

25. See Ginsberg, B., and Shefter, M. *Politics by Other Means: Politicians, Prosecutors, and the Press from Watergate to Whitewater.* New York: Norton, 1999.

26. Rauch, J. *Government's End: Why Washington Stopped Working.* New York: Public Affairs, 1999.

27. Hess, S. "Federalism and News Media to Government: Drop Dead." *Brookings Review,* Winter 2000, p. 31.

28. See Hibbing, J. R., and Theiss-Morse, E. *Congress as Public Enemy: Public Attitudes Towards American Political Institutions.* New York: Cambridge University Press, 1995, chapter three.

29. Smith (2001).

30. Farnsworth, S. J. "Federal Frustration, State Satisfaction? Voters and Decentralized Governmental Power." *Publius: The Journal of Federalism,* 1999, *23* (3), 75–88.

31. About 94 percent of Americans today own telephones, although "certain groups, such as low-income, young, and certain minority households, are still far less likely to own telephones

than higher-income, older, or White or Asian/Pacific Islander households. These disparities are particularly noticeable in rural areas." U.S. Department of Commerce, National Telecommunications and Information Administration. "Falling through the Net: Defining the Digital Divide." July 1999. www.ntia.doc.gov/ntiahome/fttn99/contents.html. See also U.S. Department of Commerce, National Telecommunications and Information Administration. "Falling through the Net: Toward Digital Inclusion." October 2000. http://search.ntia.doc.gov/pdf/fttn00.pdf.

John D. Nugent is an assistant professor in government at Connecticut College.

The Politics of E-Gov:
The Upcoming Struggle for
Redefining Civic Engagement

Costis Toregas

A lot has been said about e-government, or "e-gov," and many efforts have been made to sell government on its benefits. However, there does not seem to be a good, widely shared definition of what e-gov is, or more important what it can be. A workable definition should encompass the variety of information and telecommunication technologies through which a government can connect directly with its citizens and enhance service delivery, provide sustainable economic development, and safeguard democracy.

The service-delivery (and to a lesser degree economic-development) dimensions of e-gov have already been much discussed. The ability to pay a parking ticket or taxes on line, register for a variety of governmental programs, and link to an institution that is far away are all within the reach of governments and the information technology (IT) community today. But the democracy aspects of e-gov are more obscure and difficult to pinpoint. These aspects are the topic of this article.

The United States is a representative democracy (if one discounts the voices of despair that criticize the slippery slope of "democracy by referendum" so active in the Western states of the country). Still, the ability to establish one-to-one, one-to-many, and many-to-many communication paths may engender forms of direct, participatory democracy that could ultimately marginalize or even replace the elected official. Although only an extrapolation from present capabilities, nevertheless this possibility should encourage us to be mindful of both the public's frustration with traditional models of involvement and the potential of e-gov to provide alternative, more effective approaches.

Whatever the ultimate effect on our form of government, one thing seems likely: the comparative ease with which e-gov makes it possible for a citizen to contact a government official will result in profuse expression of opinion and concern.

The existing governmental system is not set up to manage the potential for conflict in this situation or to find ways to absorb the potential enthusiasm of an online citizenry. If there is conflict, the outcome could be a dampening of the positive forces that the new e-gov potential brings to our civic engagement landscape.

To look at this issue systematically, let us approach it like any other system: by looking at its inputs, the process acting on and transforming the inputs, and the outputs that are produced.

The Inputs

On the input side, the democratic process starts with citizens and how they can be engaged. E-gov does have new and intriguing ways in which to engage the citizen, through a computer keyboard or an interactive kiosk screen. There are advantages: uniformity of process, twenty-four/seven availability, and the capacity to record and store information for easy retrieval. But are there negatives? Well, for openers, you have to own a computer, be able to navigate screens and understand how to use the appropriate commands, and feel comfortable with the technology of telecommunications. These requirements create a barrier to access that tends to fall disproportionately on the poor and uneducated. This digital divide is a detriment to wholesale embrace of e-gov as a truly democratic technology. There are ways to lessen its impact, of course, such as placing computer terminals in libraries and kiosks in shopping malls, and developing literacy centers at the neighborhood level. But these solutions have become somewhat harder to finance and implement now that scrutiny of IT investment is more penetrating than ever.

In addition to overcoming the digital divide, full access to e-gov requires an effective telecommunications infrastructure. Here an important difference between e-gov and other "e's" becomes apparent. The requirements for e-procurement (or more generally e-business) have driven development of high-speed networks in technologically advanced areas of the country. But there is another sort of digital divide: a lack of the necessary telecommunications infrastructure, whether in a rural area, a small community, or the inner city. Without infrastructure, even a well-educated and ready-to-plug-in citizen cannot participate in what e-gov makes possible, thus blunting the potential of e-democracy as a system of developing collective action for all.

A final obstacle to citizen participation in e-gov concerns the nature of the "input." An individual who telephones or appears at the office of a political figure has to make a personal effort to present his or her case or idea. The convenience and ease of e-mail makes it possible for one person, properly trained, to flood the office of any elected official—or thousands of them—with viewpoint or venom at a click of the mouse. Anyone can get a bogus ID on an e-mail system for free, and since we have no requirement for identifying e-mail senders a politician could be literally overwhelmed with countless messages emanating in fact from the same person. The "sophistication" of the electorate's message (*sophistication* being used here in the wine-altering sense, that is, adulteration) could upend the delicate balance between citizen and representative.

Taken together, these observations point up a mismatch between the technological requirements and capacity of e-gov and the existence of appropriate rules and procedures in our political system of governance. This imbalance could easily retard, if not thwart altogether, successful introduction of this promising technology. We need to take a hard look at all the ways in which we have defined the rules of engagement between citizens and their government. For example, statistically valid online polls could become recognized as a legitimate way to measure citizen preferences. The concept of an "open meeting" could be extended to include simultaneous viewing of information by thousands of people and solicitation of reactions along carefully prescribed dimensions. Evaluation of public policy alternatives could be routinely put to an e-vote, and the "you don't need to know" argument found so infuriating by citizen advocates confronting the political or administrative process could be reversed to "come in and help us in our e-gov dialogue."

The Process

The current process through which we hear citizens' voices and convert them into political action is complex and replete with significant regional variation that highlights cultural differences going back generations. E-gov's potential for enhancing or eroding this complex process can be illustrated by the example of the open meeting. The requirement that a public deliberative body have open meetings is intended in part to guarantee that information available to one party is available to all. What would a parallel requirement look like in an e-gov environment? It could be that the whole notion of a physical meeting is quickly discarded in favor of a cybermeeting. Those who hold information or are able to process it quickly and in an automated manner could hold sway over everyone else. And what of public input? If a modest portion, let's say 0.1 percent, of a city's population decide to make their views known on a topic, then for a city of one hundred thousand this generates one hundred submissions. During a heated debate of an issue in a cybermeeting, who would read a hundred documents, let alone evaluate them and take them into account in making a final decision?

There are already a number of e-gov technology tools encroaching on (or enriching) the intent of public meetings. Listservs, chat rooms, threaded e-mails, and full portals all give citizens and their plugged-in officials a way to communicate and deliberate facelessly. This is not inherently bad since this manner of communicating should, for example, allow prior notification requirements for meetings to be met expeditiously. However, the ability to manage simultaneous information flow from hundreds of individuals is simply not available today. This should be a sobering thought for those who rush to implement e-democracy.

The Outcome

Direct participation in the democratic process (once the digital divide issues have been satisfactorily addressed) could instill new vitality into the political system. The global reach of the Internet and of telecommunications systems in general could guarantee a worldwide stage for the government using e-gov tools, bringing the benefits of trade as well as the fruits of intellectual dialogue across boundaries into every community and state. The mayor or a county commissioner in a one-paper (or one-TV-station) town could develop alternate methods of informing the people about critical, collective choices that have to be made. Finally, the service delivery aspect of e-gov might enhance the dialogue between labor and management. As citizens learn to search for and act on their own need for information and service using e-gov tools, the staffing patterns of government will change to reflect these advantages, thereby altering the role of government in the workforce.

Some Tentative Conclusions

If e-gov is successfully implemented at the local, state, and federal levels on a broad enough scale under the generous definition offered in this article, the political process may well be redefined. A new kind of politician (or a "'Netician," who represents an Internet-oriented aggregation of people rather than a geographically defined polis) may emerge who is able to interpret and act on the desires of the empowered citizen. Possession of skills such as parsing thousands of e-mails to find a pattern of common concern, or forming an Internet-based alliance to respond to issues, or thinking beyond the geopolitical boundaries of city and state to encompass an ever-shifting regional or interest-defined society of people may well become the norm.

This projection is reminiscent of the Athenian model of democracy under which citizens assembled to hear opposing arguments and then made decisions for the collective good (and for the good of those who did not have the vote). The direct participation of an informed citizenship that hears opposing views and then decides for the many is technologically available to us today. The systems and policies are not there yet, but some day they will be. Who will shape the new political systems that depend on e-gov as a foundation? Will it be the technicians who today are stitching together "killer apps" and selling them for profit? Or will it be thoughtful democrats who see the total "business process reengineering" opportunity that e-gov affords and who will step to the plate and make an effort to redefine how we construct and exercise our political machinery?

To get there, we need to rethink how our goals are and can be accomplished. The twenty-first century alliance with other institutions (so-called coopetition, or win-win alliance) will replace the classic win-lose proposition of the twentieth century. The public-private partnership under which both sides accept risk and expect financial rewards may well be the mechanism of choice. The values and principles identified in this concluding section can guide our thinking on what we want e-gov to be. People may have differing views on each value or principle, but all of these concerns have to be addressed by civic leaders in one way or another before e-gov can really become a truly comprehensive tool for civic engagement.

Sustainable Change. E-gov is a powerful engine that can rip the bolts holding it in place if attention is not paid to the rate of progress and the strategy of its introduction. The change that e-gov promotes and makes possible has to be sustainable. As for any innovation, there needs to be a champion and a solid financing plan for e-gov to work. The number of people who want to cling to the old always vastly outnumbers those who want to bring about change. It is therefore wise to craft a careful, winnable plan and develop support for it in a manner that survives election cycles, economic downturns, and people's anxiety about change. The ability to carry on a long-term implementation effort is more important than the ability to successfully implement the first stage.

Culture. E-gov initiatives encompass a range of forms and are being implemented within a number of jurisdictions and cultural contexts. A one-solution-fits-all offering is not likely to be suitable for this multiplicity of cultural differences. What is exciting to one group is boring to another; what passes as wise government to one locale may seem foolish or dangerous to another. Anyone crafting an e-gov initiative has to recognize and accommodate the existing culture in the area in which the initiative is to be implemented. For example, a parking ticket payment application that works in the Northeastern area of the country may have aspects that make it difficult to find responsive clients or users in the West. Such differences may become more consequential as e-gov initiatives expand from administrative systems (such as collection of payments, or registrations) to people-oriented systems (complaints, citizen participation, priority setting between projects). Ultimately the answer is to craft e-gov systems that reflect the culture of the community and the organization that they serve. The role of political leaders and managers is to ensure that the fit is there.

Trust. The e-commerce revolution has taught us that people are quite willing to trust a Website or a supermarket scanner with intimate details of their personal lives so long as a faster procurement cycle or a lower price is the outcome. The trust issue arising with e-gov is far deeper and more complex than can be accommodated by the technology of a digital signature or password-protected database. Dealing with trust and guaranteeing trust in a government portal environment is an evolving issue that has to be nurtured carefully before it produces good results.

A presumption of trust is part of the context of any government-to-citizen transaction. As private vendors assume a larger role in e-gov deployment strategies, it is not necessarily true that this degree of trust automatically carries over to the private partner. But the weightiest issue regarding trust is raised by the Big Brother–like potential of e-gov. The ability to assemble a detailed profile of a citizen and the concomitant fear that information entrusted to one branch of government may be abused by another represent serious concerns for which safeguards must be developed as the pace of e-gov continues. As it stands today, the ubiquity and penetration of electronic systems should make the thoughtful citizen pause before hitting the Enter key.

Education. At a minimum, e-gov initiatives make some degree of familiarity with computers and the Internet essential for citizens, government employees, and political leaders. But there are deeper educational requirements for all participants. How can we be prepared to deal with the many points of view that are sure to flare up in a digital dialogue? Our existing systems are oriented toward single-answer conclusions, while the Internet promotes the blooming of thousands of flowers that sometimes cannot be gathered into a simple solution for all to accept.

Another impact of the Internet revolution is the growing ease with which international contact can be made and deepened. Sending an e-mail to a peer overseas or scanning the Website of a potential client is quick and inexpensive. But the globalization of governance processes may increase the need to travel abroad. As it is, trade promotion that benefits jobs locally often entails local government participation on a trade delegation. This sometimes encounters skepticism from citizens, who suspect that some of the travel is more a boon-doggle than a boon. Citizens and elected leaders encounter an array of new opportunities, and considerable political discussion is needed before consensus support emerges for new policy directives.

The promise of e-gov is significant. It can become a way for our federal, intergovernmental system to align itself around a citizen-centric model and redefine alliances for a democratic future in which every voice is heard and every resource is identified and wisely invested. But leadership and trust must be developed quickly between the citizens and political leaders of today who will shape this future before it either dies off for lack of interest or takes on ominous, nondemocratic shapes. The choice is up to each of us. Do we dare engage?

Costis Toregas is the president of Public Technology, Inc.

The Virtual State: Transforming American Government?

Jane E. Fountain

Over the course of the twentieth century, American government took on its present bureaucratic form through a series of negotiations and political processes. It seems logical to assume—and recent evidence suggests—that this structure of government will change as policy makers and public managers use the Internet and other new information technologies to reshape programs, services, agencies, and policy networks. This article lays out some of the central questions about digital government—or as I call it, the virtual state.[1] By that I mean a government in which decision makers increasingly use information technology (IT) in ways that blur the boundaries among agencies, levels of government, and the private and nonprofit sectors. What are its central features? What efficiencies can we expect from digital government? What challenges should change agents be aware of? Finally, what are some of the larger questions of governance to keep in mind as innovators build the virtual state?

American government appears to be in the early phase of significant transformation as public managers begin to use the Internet and related information technologies in ways that affect coordination, control, and communication. Many of these developments hold the potential for substantial efficiency in producing and delivering information and services. However, since new and unanticipated innovation and interaction is likely to emerge, it is difficult to predict the effects of these technologies on the deeper organizational and institutional restructuring of government.

A useful way to think about digital government operations and their effects is to distinguish among three sets of government relationships. A government-to-citizen (G2C) contact encompasses information and service flows between the government and its citizens. A government-to-business (G2B) transaction includes procurement of goods and services by government from the private sector as well as a variety of other transactions between business and government. Finally, a government-to-government (G2G) relationship characterizes the networked nature of government, including interagency and intergovernmental linkage and partnership. In all cases, the Internet and the World Wide Web make it possible to move information flow and millions of transactions from paper to a shared digital environment. To better understand this new world, it is worth noting some of the most innovative examples of the virtual state in each category. Together they suggest the breadth and depth of the changes afoot in government.

How Are Innovative Governments Using the Internet?

Innovation often begins at the state level and diffuses to federal and local government. A survey of state government Websites conducted in 2000 to identify the types of service migrating to the Web indicated that the development of electronic government is just beginning. State government agencies are adding basic information to their Websites. But the security and authentication measures required to ensure that Web-based payments become feasible and sensitive documents (such as social security benefit information and tax files) can be transferred safely over the Internet are still being developed.

The results of the survey indicate that provision of electronic government services varies widely from state to state. The median number of services provided over the Web by state government is only 4; the average is about 4.5. Only a few states offer a significantly greater number of services. Several features are common to a number of states. Although the number of services a state offers on the Web is not the only measure of the growth of digital government, it indicates strong disparity among state governments.

The most frequently occurring service, available on thirty-two state government Websites, allows a citizen to find and apply for a state government job online. The second most popular service, personal income tax "e-filing," is available in twenty-four states. State governments have been able to implement electronic filing of taxes because the Internal Revenue Service supported development of private sector solutions that states can purchase and implement. Seventeen state governments permit online renewal of motor vehicle registration, which is probably the fastest growing online service. Fifteen state government Websites allow people to order a fish and game license or permit online, although most states mail the license or permit through the postal service. Fourteen state governments have a registry of sex offenders that can be searched by the public. Thirteen state governments allow the public to order vital records, such as birth, death, and marriage certificates, online. No other online government service is available from more than ten states.

But the virtual state is much more than provision of G2C services on a government Website. Web portals, which organize and integrate government services and information (and which often link to private and nonprofit sources as well), represent vigorous use of the Web to build digital government. Access Washington, perhaps the leading state government Web portal, is part of a well-integrated strategic plan to build digital government across the entire state. Washington State's Digital Government Plan describes in detail the plans for electronic government during the next five to ten years. Strong, focused leadership within the executive branch is committed to increasing integration across state and local governments, agencies, and programs. Guidelines for coherent development of digital applications as well as incentives to promote successful implementation are being disseminated. The state is also unusual in that it has developed standards for uniform Web design and protocols to guide related business process redesign in state agencies.

At present there is no dominant model of state government Web design. Washington State's top-down, comprehensive approach differs markedly from that of most other state governments, where innovation proceeds incrementally, agency by agency, at the initiative of public entrepreneurs and innovators. The state of Georgia and a few others provide a higher number of online services than Washington. Georgia's state government Web strategy is based on a decentralized approach to digital government. Other states lead in innovative design and customization of their state government Websites. For example, North Carolina and Virginia have moved beyond a simple state portal model to create powerful interfaces to help their citizens find information and to interact with these governments.

At the municipal level, Indianapolis presents the most impressive example of electronic government. Its Web portal evinces an almost seamless integration of agency and department functions. A strong proponent of digital government, former Mayor Stephen Goldsmith wondered publicly why any citizen in the future would need to go to City Hall to transact business with local government.

At the other end, federal efforts span an impressive range of activity as well. Agency Websites have proliferated. More important, such interagency Web portals as Access America for Students, Access America for Seniors, and the U.S. Business Advisor organize data according to the interests of members of the public rather than by agency. As an adjunct to moving government information and transactions online, some agencies promote civic discourse and other public discussion on the Web.

All this innovation has important implications for cost saving—and for participation in public debate. For example, the Postal Rate Commission developed a document management system, called Operating Online, that scans information into digital form. The commission Website makes these digital files available to the public, which means that anyone with Web access can read all the documentation related to hearings. Most agencies with a regulatory mandate have developed similar online document management systems.

Like other regulatory bodies, the Postal Rate Commission is required by law to conduct hearings on all rule-making cases, such as proposals for a postal rate increase or post office closing. Conducted as a legal proceeding, rule making takes place through an extended process of discovery, cross-examination, hearings, briefs, and ultimately a recommendation to (in this instance) the Postal Board of Governors. A proposed rate increase typically requires ten months of proceedings during which citizen and business responses, or pleadings, must be filed and made available to the public. The accumulated documents may run into tens of thousands of pages. Reproduced perhaps 150 times for dissemination to interested parties, the total could amount to millions of printed pages. Clearly, the ability to place information on a Website for immediate access by the public changes the internal operation of an agency and its costs, not to mention the effect it has on public access and ability to comment during the rule-making process.

Clerical staff manage the voluminous file, called a docket, containing all information related to a proposed rule—public comment, petitions, extensions, and adjudications—during the process. In 1993, the federal Department of Transportation, whose rule-making responsibilities range from air bag regulations to hazardous materials transport, managed nine docket rooms. Researching a docket was labor-intensive and costly. There was no capacity to track materials, some of which might be lost during the complex proceedings. The department moved its docket management process to the Web, making public access considerably easier. In 1999, during the rule-making process initiated when the Maritime Administration was deciding whether to reregister under a foreign flag eight ships designed to transport liquefied natural gas, the Website received more than twelve thousand hits from the firms petitioning for the change and the crew members whose jobs might be lost or modified.

Although the types of G2C innovation detailed here are strategically important, governments have been slow thus far to market new Web-based services to the public. On the one hand, they fear alienating voters who are without access to the Internet. On the other hand, such services might create a level of demand that new, relatively untested online operations may not be ready to meet. The results of a survey of state information resource executives indicate that a number of state governments have begun to take measures to motivate constituents to use new digital government features.[2] This development should proceed in tandem with maintenance of traditional service delivery methods and with an eye to meeting uncertain demand characteristics.

Regardless of complex management challenges, however, cost savings are potentially enormous. A government that offers electronic services online reaps efficiencies by generating less paperwork, decreasing the cost of processing routine transactions and lowering the error rate (whose correction requires additional work). Government employees may handle fewer inquiries for routine information. But a poorly designed Website and information in language that is difficult to understand almost certainly result in more telephone calls to the public agency. Citizens and business firms should find that the cost of compliance is decreased, including costs associated with information search, travel, waiting in line, repetitive entry of information, and errors.

G2B innovation signals new opportunity for efficiency gains in procurement and other business-government relations. The federal government spends approximately $524 billion a year, or about 6.04 percent of GDP (in 1999 dollars), on procurement operations.[3] Between 1995 and 1999, these procurement expenditures totaled $2.621 trillion. Web-based procurement operations have the potential to generate vast savings over the cost of traditional manual operations. Such operations may also increase the efficiency of the procurement process itself as new methods and business processes are developed to connect buyer and seller. Finally, a well-designed online process would increase the transparency of government procurement and markets, thereby increasing the effectiveness of regulation and enforcement.

The state of Massachusetts is actively pursuing a regional procurement consortium, called EMall, a joint program of the state's Information Technology Division, the Office of the State Comptroller, and the Operational Services Division. The consortium will include the 154 departments of the government of the Commonwealth as well as many statewide commodity contracts. Moreover, EMall states on its Website that the consortium will be open to participation from "all eligible public entities including cities and towns, public and quasi-public authorities, UFR-qualified [Uniform Financial Standards and Independent Auditor's Report] human service providers, state institutions of higher education, and other states."[4]

In an evaluative study, the designers of the online procurement system estimated the operational costs for one procurement operation. The paper-based procurement operation took 530 minutes to complete and cost $221. Using electronic data interchange (EDI), a precursor to use of the Internet and Web, required 240 minutes and cost $100 to complete the same procurement transaction. Web-based procurement as it is designed in EMall required only 49 minutes and cost $21. Consortium development of state government digital procurement makes sense because the start-up costs involved in building such a complex system are high enough to dissuade many state legislatures from appropriating funds. Pooling resources for such a venture may not only speed implementation but also contribute to economies of scale in purchasing and the opportunity for related network activity.

G2G efforts encompass several types of relationship among government agencies, ranging from data sharing to interagency partnership and networks that link internal operations across jurisdictions. A well-functioning interagency Web portal requires back-end integration and significant cooperation (or social capital) within a network of agencies and programs.[5] G2G developments are currently constrained by institutional arrangements such as oversight and budget processes that tend to favor single-agency activity. In addition, the administrative independence of federal, state, and local governments means that an executive is attuned to the political constituents in that operating environment. Equally important, legal restrictions prohibit information sharing in some key organizations, for example, the Internal Revenue Service and the Social Security Administration.

It is difficult to forecast the economic impact of G2G activity. Clearly, partnership and shared databases could help the public and government avoid duplication of information gathering, updating, and storage; reduce mailing and other costs of distributing information on paper; and save time and resources in hundreds of ways by enhancing efficiency of operation and service delivery. In the current political environment, which still favors shrinking the size of government by reducing the number of government employees, it is highly likely that G2G initiatives will be used for further downsizing.

Yet in spite of obstacles and the traditional difficulty of interagency coordination, a surprising and growing number of partnerships suggests readiness and ability on the part of government executives to explore the benefits of G2G activity. Interagency partnership and networks can afford cost savings. More important, however, they offer the potential for government to solve otherwise intractable policy problems that fall inherently between agency boundaries.[6]

An example of an interagency information sharing effort with strong leverage, the Information Network for Public Health Officials (which is housed at the Centers for Disease Control and Protection, U.S. Public Health Service), connects federal, state, and community-level public health practitioners. The information network gives public health professionals the ability to access a shared national collection of public health data and information. The network decreases fragmentation in public health service provision by diminishing geographic and bureaucratic barriers. It links federal, state, and local practitioners and allows them to exchange data and information over the Web. The ability to communicate easily in this networked environment has helped a broad, geographically dispersed group build consensus around the benefits of strengthening shared infrastructure of this type. Public health workers gained appreciation for the importance of G2G sharing, and the potential of such projects, as they used the online tools in early versions of the network.

These examples of G2C, G2B, and G2G innovation demonstrate clearly that the virtual state entails much more than government putting information on the Web for access by the public. Some of the broad estimates of savings are impressive. The use of e-mail alone has been estimated by Ferris Research to generate an average annual savings of $9,000 per office worker, or a productivity gain of 15 percent.[7] Ferris calculated that this typical office worker saves, on average, 381 hours per year by using e-mail. The study even factored in nonproductive use of e-mail, estimating it at 115 hours per worker. The U.S. Department of Commerce has estimated that paper-based, traditional processing of the payments that flow into its offices costs between $1.65 and 2.70 for each transaction, compared to $0.60 to $1.00 for Web-based processing. As noted earlier, expanded use of information-based technology reduces the hidden cost that individuals incur in dealing with the government. For example, the U.S. Office of Management and Budget estimates that businesses and individual taxpayers spend 6.1 billion hours annually in complying with federal tax law. Reckoning this time at $30 per hour produces a total of $183 billion per year. Similarly, the Tax Foundation and the U.S. General Accounting Office estimate compliance costs of 15 and 19 percent, respectively, of income tax collected.[8]

The potential efficiency gains alone should stimulate government executives to launch digital government projects. The estimated savings that could be realized have galvanized an industry of e-government vendors who are soliciting projects as government outsourcing increases. Cost savings and the benefits of increased public access to information and services, however, represent only a small subset of the promise of digital government. More important, however, is public dialogue about how digital government will be designed and implemented. The central issues are democratic in nature, rather than simply economic. How are conceptions of public service changing? How will dramatic modifications of access affect rates and types of civic participation? How will reliance on the public sector for design, implementation, and management of digital government affect the traditional boundaries between what is public and what is private? These are just a few of the pressing questions that move discussion of digital government beyond its economic importance to its broader implications for democracy.

The Challenges That Lie Ahead

The promise of the virtual state comes with considerable challenges that government decision makers and concerned citizens will face during the next decade of rapid development. Beyond simply developing the requisite infrastructure to handle the growth of electronic government, there is the need to guarantee equitable access for all citizens, and the obligation to safeguard individual privacy and ensure the security of transactions. Additionally, a host of governance issues, such as normative concerns about the appropriate role of the public and private sectors in developing and managing the public's information, will be encountered.

As of 1999, the distance between information haves and have-nots was growing rather than shrinking. Those who live in households with income of $75,000 or more and located in an urban area are more than nine times as likely to have a personal computer in their home, and approximately twenty times more likely to have Internet access than those who live in a low-income household. Racial and ethnic disparities persist: an African American or Latino household in the United States is 40 percent as likely to have Internet access as a white household.[9] Use of the Internet is correlated with an individual's ethnicity; race; age; income; and proximity to major business, technological and decision-making regions. As a sample of geographic disparity in access, just over 50 percent of those living in Washington, D.C., San Francisco, Austin, and Seattle/Tacoma currently use the Internet—but only one third or fewer of those who live in cities such as Pittsburgh, Tulsa, Birmingham, and Charleston/Huntington (West Virginia) use it.

Inequality of Internet access and use remains a fundamental problem to be addressed as decision makers allocate funds to build the virtual state. The cost savings of digital government are tied to the percentage of the public that will use the Internet in their interaction with government. In the near term, government agencies have to maintain a dual capacity, managing both traditional and Web-based operations. Recent research suggests that in a political environment where the citizen is increasingly viewed as a customer, the wealthy customer may receive better treatment as digital government architectures are designed and implemented.[10] If this is the case throughout government, then enacting technology with a customer focus and without conscious effort to reduce inequality may exacerbate the digital divide.

An increasingly digital government favors those with access to a computer and the Internet and the skills to use these sophisticated tools competently. Text-based service delivery over the Internet assumes literacy (and, typically, proficiency in English). Moreover, the complexity and enormous volume of government information on the Web requires people who use it to develop the skills needed to search for information and evaluate the output of search tools. Ironically, the very people who are poorly equipped to use digital government services may find themselves monitored by tools that are in fact Web-based, as health care providers, case officers for welfare and other entitlement programs, and criminal justice personnel increasingly collect and integrate personal information to aid decision making.

Another challenge derives from the enormous tasks of infrastructure building that lie ahead. The technical infrastructure required to build a virtual state is still in its early development in much of the country. Estimates of cost savings assume sufficient capacity to handle volume and high-speed Internet access and transmission. Transaction time also affects the reliability of digital government transactions and is, for this reason, a key element of building trust and security in these systems. The time required to transfer a ten megabyte file, roughly equal to the contents of six or seven floppy disks, varies from eight seconds to forty-six minutes depending upon the sophistication of the connection. Many legacy computer systems used in governments throughout the United States were not built for the interactivity of a Web-based application, or for the transaction volume envisioned in digital government.

In theory, a government agency can transfer enormous amounts of data in seconds, saving government and the public time and money. In practice, efficiency depends on several factors: the type of technology the public agency uses to connect to the Internet, the policies government decision makers develop to guide data sharing and transfer, and a growing number of security and privacy issues.[11] Given current stringency in most government budgets, funding for information infrastructure remains a serious impediment to developing digital government.

Privacy and security loom as urgent and important policy issues as government moves toward a greater level of online interactivity with the public, including transfer of funds and private information such as that found in tax returns, financial aid applications, medical histories, and social security filings. Information systems are vulnerable to white collar criminals, hackers, and thousands of "bugs" or errors in computer programs that have been patched together during several decades of incremental, at times poorly documented, system development. Increasing networked connection also increases the vulnerability of information systems to power outage, sabotage, and unanticipated problems in tightly coupled, interdependent computerized systems.[12]

A third set of challenges relates to governance using new information tools and institutional structures whose features differ from the bureaucratic state of the twentieth century. Web-based and organizational networks are not yet so extensive as to give the public manager anything more than a foretaste of what may be coming. Eventually, boundaries in cyberspace and in organizational networks may become as important as the traditional bureaucratic boundaries within which a public agency has traditionally operated. What will be the impact on public management in these new governance structures? An outline is beginning to emerge from innovations around the country.

Public executives and managers in a networked environment can no longer afford the luxury of relegating technology matters to technical staff. Many issues that appear to be exclusively technical are also deeply political and strategic in nature. In some cases, new use of technology furthers an existing agency or program mission. But in others, using the Internet can play a transformative role and lead to expansion or rethinking of mission and change in internal and external boundaries, accountability, and jurisdiction.

The rules of the game in public management have long rewarded agency-specific endeavors. Agency autonomy protects the integrity of policy areas, programs, and clients through clear jurisdiction, line items in the budget, and procedures for accountability. Success in a government agency has often meant increasing (or at least maintaining) program budgets, staff, and other resources. Internal agency conflict could be solved, reconciled, or dampened through bureaucratic governance structures and processes.

The rules of the game for the manager in a networked environment—the sort that increasingly accompanies digital government—are different. Partnership across jurisdictional boundaries requires cooperative behavior and the ability to coordinate, often without a clear governance structure. Many of the advantages of the Internet come from building interorganizational networks, a process that requires considerable executive leadership and skill. One of the challenges now facing the government executive is that multiple rules and multiple games are currently in play, each of which possesses its own internal logic.

Executives must master the technological game if they are to use the Internet strategically rather than simply following fashion, contractors, or the lead of a best-practice agency in their field. In addition, the public manager must remain an astute player of the bureaucratic game, while also becoming proficient at the network game so as to establish productive and useful partnerships in a time of scarce and diminishing resources in government. Public service has never been more challenging; as a virtual state is being developed, it has rarely been more exciting or important.

Increasing use of the Internet is creating a network society and networked government. But close examination of current organizations and institutions reveals that many potentially useful connections remain unforged, and numerous opportunities to gain prospectively stunning efficiency or to build joint problem solving capacity in complex policy areas remain unexplored. The Internet is often used to reinforce an old institutional structure rather than open the possibility for innovative public service.

Some experienced political actors downplay the significance of contemporary technological change by arguing that politics will not change in a digital environment.[13] Although it seems likely that technological change as significant as that enabled by the Internet will lead to deep structural change in government, the degree of its impact on politics is open to reasoned disagreement. Too few analyses of digital government treat technology and politics with equal seriousness. In most treatments of digital government, technology is viewed as if it alone would usher in a transformation of the state and as if politics and current institutions could be ignored in such a transformation.

An important series of questions for governance relates to the nature of the public-private policy network and the roles of the public and private sectors in designing, developing, managing, and controlling the virtual state. Economic incentives in the private sector help to generate rapid, innovative solutions and applications that are highly beneficial for government. Private sector vendors of digital government, along with professional service firms, have aggressively targeted construction and operation of the virtual state as an enormous and lucrative market to be tapped.

But information architecture, both hardware and software, is more than a technical instrument; it is a powerful form of governance. As a consequence, outsourcing information architecture and operations is, effectively, outsourcing of policy making. Public servants and others who hold the public trust bear grave responsibility to forge long-term policy that guards the interest of citizens and that protects the integrity of citizen data and public information. The responsibility may make governments seem slower moving than the private sector, lacking in strategic power, or unsophisticated relative to best practices in the economy. But as we build a virtual state, public servants are needed more than ever to guard the public interest.

Notes

1. The author gratefully acknowledges the support of the Visions Project of the Kennedy School of Government at Harvard University, the Brookings Institution, and the Internet Policy Institute for support of the author's research on digital government. For a detailed examination of the research, data, and policy implications presented in this article, see Fountain, J. E. *Building the Virtual State: Information Technology and Institutional Change.* Washington, D.C.: Brookings Institution Press, 2001.

2. National Association of State Information Resource Executives. "Information Security in State Government Information Technology." (Report.) Lexington, Ky.: National Association of State Information Resource Executives [now NASCIO], 1999.

3. U.S. Department of Commerce. "Real Government Consumption Expenditures and Gross Investment by Type." Washington, D.C.: U.S. Government Printing Office.

4. www.state.ma.us/emall.

5. See Fountain, J. E. "Social Capital: A Key Enabler of Innovation." In L. M. Branscomb and J. H. Keller (eds.), *Investing in Innovation: Creating a Research and Innovation Policy That Works.* Cambridge, Mass.: MIT Press, 1998.

6. Bardach, E. *Getting Agencies to Work Together: The Practice and Theory of Managerial Craftsmanship. Washington, D.C.: Brookings Institution Press, 1998.*

7. Ferris Research. "Quantifying the Productivity Gains of Email." In L. Schroeder, "Ferris Research Shows That Company Policies on Email Use Can Measurably Improve Staff Productivity." (FR-109.) San Francisco, Jan. 18, 2000.

8. U.S. Senate. *Tax Complexity Fact Book 2000;* Slemrod, J. "The Simplification Potential of Alternatives to the Income Tax." *Tax Notes,* Feb. 27, 1995.

9. National Telecommunications and Information Administration. *Falling Through the Net: Defining the Digital Divide.* Washington, D.C.: NTIA, 1999.

10. Fountain (2001).

11. See, for example, U.S. General Accounting Office. "Information Security: Serious and Widespread Weaknesses Persist at Federal Agencies." Sept. 2000 (www.gao.gov/new.items/ai00295.pdf); and "Internet Privacy: Comparison of Federal Agency Practices with FTC's Fair Information Principles." Sept. 2000 (www.gao.gov/new.items/ai00296r.pdf).

12. Rochlin, G. *Trapped in the Net: The Unanticipated Consequences of Computerization.* Princeton, N.J.: Princeton University Press, 1997.

13. See, for example, Darman, R., "Reflections on 'The Virtual State'" and Burke, S., "Some Cautionary Notes on the 'Virtual State,'" both in E. C. Kamarck and J. S. Nye, Jr. (eds.), *Democracy.com: Governance in a Networked World.* Hollis, N.H.: Hollis Press, 1999.

Jane E. Fountain is an associate professor of public policy at the John F. Kennedy School of Government.

CitiStat and the Baltimore Neighborhood Indicators Alliance: Using Information to Improve Communication and Community

Marsha R. B. Schachtel

Baltimore, a postindustrial city on the brink of a renaissance, offers a lesson about the challenges and promise of using information to improve public services and build community. Advances in technology are enabling local government and citizens to collect and use information systematically to enhance communication and improve governance.

At the heart of community building are the individuals, the groups, the institutions, and the corporations (both for-profit and nonprofit) that take responsibility for making positive change in the places they call home. In what many say is a survival response to the failings of their governments,[1] over the past two decades communities have matured in their ability and willingness to tackle tough challenges. In the process, individual citizens have found themselves empowered and become more self-reliant.

Simultaneously, local governments, particularly in cities, have concluded that they cannot govern for the people but must govern with them. Baltimore Mayor Martin O'Malley's neighborhood strategy starts with basic principles—not only that "Baltimore's city government will provide a basic level of service to improve the quality of life in every neighborhood" but also that "community development is not just the city government's responsibility"; "city government will support neighborhood leaders who are working to help themselves"; and "city government will take a market-based approach to community development, which builds from strengths and takes advantage of unique opportunities."[2] In short, citizens are no longer clients of government but partners.

The partners share needs for high-quality, timely information that enables them to

1. Assess strengths and needs on a variety of interrelated factors
2. Weigh alternative courses of action
3. Develop strategies
4. Develop tactical plans, including appropriate action by various public, private, and nonprofit partners
5. Manage implementation
6. Assess results of their own action and that of others
7. Make midcourse corrections

Technical advances and cost reduction in computer hardware, address-matching and GIS (geographic information system) software, and availability of automated administrative data have put new information tools within the reach of many of the partners.[3]

CitiStat

Baltimore first embraced geographically linked information technology to aggressively fight crime. Mayor O'Malley had made public safety the cornerstone of his election campaign, arguing that it was essential for restoring the quality of life in Baltimore's neighborhoods and building investor confidence, and that it could be enhanced through local action. He adopted Jack Maple's Comstat approach (creating a computerized database to track crime incidence by time and location), which had been credited with dramatic reductions in crime in New York, New Orleans, and other cities. After similarly positive results began to take shape in Baltimore, the mayor asked whether Comstat techniques could be applied to improve management of other city services. He foresaw that if comparable results could be realized, they would generate (1) immediate savings for a cash-starved city treasury; (2) enhanced confidence on the part of citizen taxpayers and state and federal government grant providers that the city was a competent steward of resources entrusted to it; and (3) better-quality services that enhanced quality of life, leading to more investment by residents and businesses. With these goals in mind, CitiStat was born.

At the heart of Comstat and CitiStat is "accurate and timely intelligence," the first tenet of Jack Maple's canon. Much of the public attention to these initiatives has been attracted by highly detailed maps of everything from burglaries to potholes, vacant houses, lead paint poisoning, and rat concentrations. These maps reveal the scope of problems and citizens' need for city response street by street, neighborhood by neighborhood.

It is the geocoded data behind the maps, however, tied to payroll information in mundane computer-generated spreadsheets, that enables the mayor; top deputies; and the heads of the law, labor, and finance departments to evaluate the efficiency of the city's response to citizen needs. These top-level personnel are able to see patterns of absenteeism, overtime use, and productivity.

Biweekly meetings with each agency are an opportunity to use the data, analyzed by the CitiStat staff, to execute the other three elements of the Comstat/CitiStat approach: (1) rapid deployment of resources, (2) effective tactics and strategies, and (3) relentless follow-up and assessment.

Eight major departments or divisions now report to the mayor and his team every two weeks at one-hour CitiStat sessions, including those having the most direct effect on the quality of life in a community: housing and community development, health, fire, recreation and parks, sanitation, water and waste water, transportation, and general services. There are plans to add education, social services, and finance.

An early and abiding objective of CitiStat is to control overtime costs. It became clear that unanticipated absenteeism contributed significantly to overtime needs, so all types of leave are now monitored closely. For each unit within each department, overtime, leave, disability days, and light-duty days are tracked and compared to the previous two-week period. Tighter management and changes in personnel policy suggested in the meetings have been credited with reducing overtime use. Building on the experience of Mayor Edward Rendell in Philadelphia and the recommendations of a Baltimore business leaders' task force, fleet management was also targeted for tighter management and savings.

Productivity in each department, unit, and team is measured in units appropriate to function. The variables tracked have evolved over time; others are added as issues are brought to the attention of the mayor's office. This occurs through a variety of channels: "mayor's night in" sessions, community meetings, deputy mayors, the mayor's Office of Neighborhoods, and conversations with city council members. Some elements formerly measured were dropped when it became apparent they were not useful indicators of problems or performance. The functional data tracked for each agency are listed in Table 1.

At the CitiStat meetings, the first deputy mayor uses the data as a point of departure to call on managers to explain trends, describe incidents, and then speculate on broader issues of which the incidents may be a symptom. Even a fairly sedate meeting on water and waste water can showcase the potential contribution of the CitiStat program. In a recent meeting, a second water main break in a one-block area raised questions of whether earlier repairs might have damaged the fragile pipes. Tracking the results of maintenance operations identifies problems with aging pipes and targets them for more extensive repair.

The meetings have been designed to avoid what was believed to be an adversarial "gotcha" atmosphere of the Comstat model. They are an opportunity for on-the-spot problem solving, with most relevant decision makers present. Citizen complaints about loose steel plates over roadway repair holes led to a carefully mapped inventory and identification of contractors who were responsible. The director of public works then notified contractors that they would be fined $50 per day if the plates were not properly secured or removed as scheduled. A quick CitiStat conversation among the city's law and finance

Table 1. Agencies Participating in the CitiStat Program

Agency	Data Tracked
Housing and Community Development	• Complaints: vacant buildings, exteriors, maintenance, trash and cans, rodents and insects, miscellaneous; new, resolved, pending inspection (by district) • Cleaning and boarding: work orders created, outstanding, and completed for city-owned and private properties (by district) • Housing inspection: days worked, total inspections, daily average, number of inspectors (by district, by inspector grade, e.g., I, II, III); court cases, abatements, citations • Plans and examining: total plans reviewed, time required, backlog (by category of plan) • Construction and building inspection: electrical, mechanical, building inspections each period • Property acquisition: number of acquisitions by type, activity, average acquisition time • Human service programs: applications received, certified, awaiting certification, pending information, denied
Recreation and Parks	• Recreation centers: enrollment, average daily attendance, revenue generated, volunteers (by center) • Parks: applications, permits issued, revenue (by park) • City farms: plots, revenue (by park) • Pools: attendance, revenue (by pool) • Youth and adult sports: number of teams, attendance, revenue (by sport) • Senior citizens: enrollment and attendance (by activity) • Special facilities (golf, soccer, skating, other): activity level, revenue (by facility)
Health	• Environmental health: food investigation, childhood lead poisoning investigation, animal complaints, child care facility inspection (by inspector, district, citations, abatements) • Health services: clinics for men, dentistry, STD, TB, family planning, healthy teens and young adults, school-based (number of patient visits, number of unduplicated patients, average wait time) • Clients in methadone service by program (percentage active after one, three, or six months; capacity; average number of active clients; number of urinalyses and percentage positive; average length of stay; ASI medical, employment, drug, alcohol, legal, family, psychiatric) • Increase in number of pregnant women and children applying for health benefits • Adolescent and child health: immunization; referral to maternal and infant nursing; vision, hearing, and scoliosis screening • Cancer detection: Pap test, breast and cervical cancer screening
DPW, Solid Waste	• Citizen complaints: dirty alleys and lots, mixed refuse, recycling, bulk trash, illegal dumping, corner cans, rats, miscellaneous

- Refuse: mixed refuse collection, recycling collection, bulk trash, alley and lot cleaning, mechanical street sweeping, rat eradication; number of routes, employees required, lost man-days, average tons per route, average time per route, overtime per route, complaints received and abated (by territory and supervisor name)
- Sanitation enforcement: days worked, total and average daily number of citations issued, monetary assessments, lost man-days (by assigned work area and supervisor)

DPW, Water and Waste Water	<ul><li>Meter reading: staffing, lost workdays, average number of daily readings (by sector and supervisor)</li><li>Maintenance work orders: Prior backlog, new work orders, abated, average abatement days (by unit: meter shop, billing request, water, sewer, storm water maintenance)</li><li>Capital improvement status: schedule status, contract amount, contractor name, engineer name, project manager, number and amount of extra work orders, project address (for each project)</li></ul>
DPW, Transportation	<ul><li>Maintenance: work order backlog, created, abated; average abatement time for streets, roads, and alleys; signs, street markings, signals, lot cleaning and grass cutting, street lighting, forestry, conducts, parking meters, snow, miscellaneous (by crew, percentage abated within forty-eight hours)</li><li>Potholes: number filled, complaint abatement rate, daily average (by sector)</li><li>Parking enforcement: days worked, citations issued per day (by supervisor)</li><li>Capital improvement status: schedule status, contract amount, number and amount of extra work orders, contractor name, project manager (for each project, delayed projects highlighted)</li></ul>
DPW, General Services	<ul><li>Fleet management: vehicle inventory, availability, utilization, accidents, repairs, fuel utilization (by vehicle type, agency)</li></ul>
Fire Department	<ul><li>Fire suppression: 911 service calls, residential structure fires, nonresidential structure fires, nonstructure fires, HAZMAT incidents, mutual aid incidents in neighboring jurisdictions, false alarms, private alarms, average response time (by engine and truck company, by HAZMAT unit)</li><li>Fire deaths: civilian and firefighter deaths, arson-related deaths, type of structure, deaths in structures with and without working smoke detector</li><li>Emergency medical services: 911 EMS service calls, runs, transport, response time, billings, revenue collected, collection rate (by engine and truck company, by medic unit)</li><li>Fire prevention and investigation: public fire safety education, number of individuals reached, number of community meetings and events, inspections, permits issued, smoke detectors distributed and installed, investigations, investigation-related criminal arrests (by engine and truck company)</li></ul>

department representatives resulted in an enforcement plan and an agenda item for the next meeting to check on implementation progress.

Baltimore has also taken the first steps toward what systems integrators call "front end automation." Using a contractor to field, electronically record, and channel complaints made to a special telephone hotline and e-mail address, the mayor was able to offer a forty-eight-hour pothole guarantee. In the first two weeks, five hundred complaints were received, of which 96.6 percent were fixed within two business days. This is a first step toward a full-service one-call center to handle all citizen complaints, to simplify citizen access, reduce paperwork, improve responsiveness, and by analyzing repeat complaints improve independent monitoring of actual abatement performance by agencies.

The promise of the CitiStat technique for tackling multifaceted, interdepartmental, intergovernmental challenges is beginning to be realized. Spearheaded by Baltimore's City Health Department, LeadStat is being used to guide and manage the mayor's initiative on lead poisoning prevention. A linked GIS-capable database was developed and is being used for mass code enforcement and improved coordination of actions on city properties as well as planning and policy. The city departments of health and housing have cross-trained their inspectors, and joint inspection of homes with lead violations has begun. Coordination with the state's Department of the Environment has been improved. More than 120 cases were filed in the first year of the initiative—after no landlord had been prosecuted in a decade. City and state legislation to tighten enforcement and screening of children was passed. Increased funding from the state Department of Housing and Community Development and the Empower Baltimore Management Corporation is being used to implement phase two of the initiative, which coordinates abatement, demolition, relocation, prevention, testing, and outreach as well as enforcement. Comparison of the January 1, 2000, base map with the latest updated actions in February 2001 shows a dramatic reduction in active lead violations (www.baltimorecity.gov/government/health/leadstat/index.html). Similar efforts are being undertaken to coordinate a partnership of multiple city and state agencies with thirty faith institutions aimed at reducing youth violence, and geographically targeted redevelopment efforts on the east and west sides.

CitiStat has marked a number of accomplishments since it began in June 2000[4]:

- $1.2 million in Department of Public Works (DPW) overtime savings were achieved in the first five months of FY2001.
- Overtime for meter readers dropped 60 percent from the first to second quarters of calendar year 2001; managers hope to eliminate all use of overtime by the fourth quarter.
- Overtime hours and overtime call backs at the fire department have dropped 70.5 percent and 78.7 percent respectively since December 2000. It is estimated that about $1.9 million will be saved in FY 2001 by these reductions.

- $2 million was saved this year through reducing fleets, selling excess city vehicles, and limiting the number of cars taken home by employees.
- Fleet deployment improvements and prioritization of repairs have enabled the fire department to increase emergency medical service coverage by more than 22 percent with less than a 6 percent increase in the total number of medic units.
- Active lead violations were reduced by 25 percent.
- The number of children tested for lead for the first time rose 51 percent.
- The DPW was reorganized along geographic lines to put one handpicked, seasoned manager in charge of all solid waste services (household trash collection, street and alley cleaning, and bulk trash) within each collection "borough." The reorganization has resulted in record low rates of overtime utilization, lost workdays, and citizen complaints.
- In the first two months of implementation, change in policy to allow crews to be notified in advance which addresses have bulk trash to be picked up increased scheduled bulk trash pickups by 2.5 times and reduced missed-pickup complaints from 6.3 to 0.8 percent of all requests.
- In the first eight weeks after a notice that DPW would begin terminating service to customers with delinquent water bills, three hundred accounts were paid in full or the customer agreed to a payment plan with the city's finance department.
- Inspectors from the public works, housing, health, and fire departments meet biweekly with the Liquor Board and police department to develop strategies and coordinate tactics for problem properties in key corridors.
- Citizen help was actively recruited in identifying homes without smoke detectors when analysis of fire deaths showed that all but one occurred in a structure without a working detector.

Baltimore Neighborhood Indicators Alliance

In 1998, a group of Baltimore's local foundations, neighborhood representatives, data collectors, nonprofit providers of technical assistance to neighborhoods, city agency officials, and university staff began meeting to devise a data utility for community builders and the public, private, and nonprofit organizations that support them. The goal of the Baltimore Neighborhood Indicators Alliance (BNIA) was to create (1) a widely and easily accessible gateway to neighborhood indicators; (2) access to technical assistance in developing, interpreting, and using indicators; (3) small data partnership grants to help communities develop and use primary source data; and (4) a forum for assessing progress toward shared goals.

Modeled on organizations established by the first six members of the National Neighborhood Indicators Partnership (NNIP), in Atlanta, Boston, Cleveland, Denver, Oakland, and Providence, and aided by the Urban Institute's ongoing technical assistance and shared experiences of these pioneers,

BNIA was launched in 1999 and hired its first director in 2000. Because it started late in the information technology revolution and grew up in the context of a rich array of existing local efforts, BNIA's approach departed from those of the early NNIP cities. Incubated under the wing of the philanthropic community as a whole (the Association of Baltimore Area Grantmakers), BNIA has developed as an alliance that draws on the strengths of each partner but does not ask them to depart from their core mission.

Rather than constructing a centralized data warehouse, BNIA has adopted a technical approach that permits users to organize and "grab" data from original data sources such as the Data Collaborative's[5] extensive geocoded information on children and families, the Baltimore Ecosystems Study information on watersheds and the urban environment, and administrative data such as housing and sanitation complaints from multiple city agencies. Instead of building a large technical-assistance staff, BNIA is relying on its partners at the Enoch Pratt Free Library, the Citizens Planning and Housing Association, the Neighborhood Design Center, and the Community Resource Center at Morgan State University to help communities access data through BNIA and use them strategically to effect change. An online technical assistance toolkit is under development (www.bnia.org/trainingpage) and will include a train-the-trainers curriculum and supportive materials. Most important, community users are being asked to provide feedback to BNIA on the data they access, sharing their interpretation of why trends or conditions exist and noting any discrepancies between recorded data and conditions they see.

In addition, neighborhoods embarking on a strategic planning initiative are being assisted in efforts to collect their own data and merge it with secondary sources. An experiment that brings together an umbrella community group, the Greater Northwest Community Coalition, with the Enterprise Foundation, the Neighborhood Design Center, and BNIA is using Palm Pilots to survey building use and conditions in an area of ten thousand homes and forty thousand residents. By using city base maps, participants are producing a baseline assessment of existing assets and challenges, in a process similar to that undertaken previously in Lorain, Ohio; the Mount Pleasant neighborhood in Cleveland; and York, Pennsylvania. This information will be used to devise neighborhood improvement strategies, including enlisting city government help in attacking the most serious problems and using the asset inventory to devise a marketing campaign to attract new residents. Primary data collection activities of this type are also seen as a vehicle for organizing and mobilizing community residents.

Parallels and Potential Linkages

CitiStat and BNIA are efforts to use information to improve governance, a broader notion than government and one that involves all the elements in society that have influence over public life and economic and social development. Epstein, Wray, Marshall, and Grifel[6] believe that community improvement results from the interaction of government policy and implementation, engaged citizens, and performance management: "A government's basic approach to policy and implementation, including its budgeting, planning, and operational functions, must be competent for the government to be able to be a positive influence on the community and not just a resource drain. Performance measurement is needed to determine whether results are achieved. And citizen engagement helps assure they are results that matter to people of the community."

Information as a Tool for Collaboration. CitiStat is a management tool, part of the executive oversight function of the mayor's office. Its five-person staff gives templates to the agencies and collects and analyzes the data they submit. In addition, the staff makes highlights available to top managers, maps and graphs key indicators, and does spot checks to verify agency reporting of abated complaints. The effort, established with an initial outlay of $20,000, is relatively low-tech; the initiative does not have its own server. Most of the agencies rely on hand-entered data. Much of the data were already being collected but not marshaled usably. The data have provided a factual basis and a point of departure for discussion between line managers and top executives about performance and challenges, which in the best of circumstances leads to collaborative problem solving. Changes in policies and actions beyond the scope of a manager often hamper performance, and cooperation among heretofore "stovepiped" executives (personnel, law, finance) is necessary for improvement.

Similarly, the Urban Institute and the first neighborhood-indicator implementers have found that collaboration is made easier when new information or information in a new form can be brought to the table. This newly shared base of information helps to break down old ways of thinking about issues and enables parties with diverse points of view to jointly devise new approaches.[7]

Information has proven, in both BNIA and CitiStat, to be an aid to communication. Technology has improved the speed and clarity with which information can be accessed and shared by decision makers in government and the community. The city's role as a partner in BNIA holds the potential for improved community-building collaboration as neighbors and government view the same facts in close-to-real time and use them as the basis for discussion. Automation of data collection and entry by both city agencies and communities continues to enhance these possibilities. The new demands for information have caught city government at a difficult time, however. Years of tight budgets have left many agencies unprepared to collect or manage data. One paradox of fiscal stress is that just when they are needed most, management tools (and the administrators) are early targets for budget cutting that seeks to safeguard direct citizen services.

Information as a Tool for Policy and Program Development. CitiStat data and capabilities are just beginning to be used by the mayor's office and relevant agencies to inform policy and program development. The LeadStat initiative described earlier is the best example of how collaborative examination of micro-level data has revealed the need for new legal infrastructure and policy changes for a variety of partners. Vacant house information holds similar potential, as do the many data overlays that can be brought to discussion of area-based economic and community development strategies.

BNIA data and indicators are being developed from the outset for strategic planning purposes. The initiative grew out of the frustration experienced by community leaders as each separately sought to gain access to key neighborhood-level data held by various local, state, and federal governments to permit better understanding of the current conditions in their neighborhoods and to plan for improvement. Conversely, a community invested in collecting and analyzing data brings to it special knowledge unavailable to the independent analyst; the Urban Institute notes that "stakeholders understand nuances related to purposes, values, and unquantifiable aspects of the situation that can guide them in adjusting an analytic sequence in process to better achieve their own ends."[8]

Information-based situation assessment is the key to all policy development and is a need shared by CitiStat and BNIA. Contextual variables affect even the most basic service delivery decisions, as well as the appropriateness of strategies and programs; mapping technology has made it possible to visually appreciate patterns that might formerly have required long hours of studying columns of numbers. Although direct access to CitiStat data is limited under executive privilege, BNIA has received permission from agencies to grant access to some of the data submitted to CitiStat, including complaints related to housing, sanitation, trash, and transportation. These data can now be custom mapped by users of BNIA's online interactive maps. In return, CitiStat has tapped some of the databases that make up BNIA's virtual data warehouse, particularly when its resources are being used as the basis for discussion of a policy-related crosscutting initiative. The Data Collaborative's information on conditions of children and families has been used as a backdrop for KidStat discussions and will undoubtedly be exploited more extensively when human development agencies are added to CitiStat later in the year. Sharing of house-by-house property condition surveys conducted by neighbors and city agencies such as housing and community development, particularly if conducted using the same protocols, can extend the reach of both partners.

A key question for CitiStat is how far it should go in developing policy-related information and analysis services. Because it boasts the only complement of data analysts with cross-agency jurisdiction, CitiStat is increasingly asked to serve as a broad data integrator, pulling it away from the essential mission of management accountability. As BNIA matures, its city government partners may find that it is a useful vehicle for developing and providing such services in the same way that other neighborhood-indicator operations around the country have done for their local governments.

Information as a Tool for Implementation. CitiStat has proven to be quite useful in sparking revision in practice and monitoring the effects on key management outcomes. It is becoming clear as the initiative matures that measuring change in some health, housing, and welfare outcome indicators every two weeks is an exercise in frustration for all involved. Adjustment in the reporting schedule for some functions is being explored.

No analysis of urban issues concludes that problems can be addressed in isolation. Mapping technology has begun to give communities and city government the ability to see multiple forces at work, although the interaction among factors remains a matter of debate. CitiStat's multiagency initiatives are beginning to foster collaborative thinking across departmental lines, but at the most basic level of implementation integration occurs on the street. Until now, it has been community activists who rang the bell when one agency's inspectors went over the same ground those from another agency had trodden the day before, or when opportunities for cleaning an alley of illegal dumping and removing a cache for illegal drugs could be seized by joint police and solid-waste action. Community building has always involved thinking comprehensively about multiple, interrelated challenges and then working entrepreneurially to attack one or two high-priority issues. Successful community building efforts address problems in ways that build social and human capital, the essential ingredients of a self-confident and effective community.[9]

Full participation by the city in BNIA presents an opportunity to take the multifaceted information that CitiStat is capable of generating and use it to reinforce ongoing community self-help efforts. The area-specific teams of front-line city managers and neighborhood representatives that the mayor's Office of Neighborhoods will be establishing present an opportunity to test this approach.

Information as a Tool for Performance Management. Early CitiStat efforts have focused on basic management questions: How many vehicles do we have? How many employees are available to work? Where are they? How productive are they? Once the fundamentals were under control, the technique could be used to begin establishing benchmarks and baselines needed to measure service quality. A first question is what and how to measure progress toward community improvement. In the process of creating the BNIA, a scan of communities' strategic plans was conducted. This review revealed that it is possible for a diverse collection of neighborhoods to come to a consensus about concrete targets. Operation Reach Out Southwest, an umbrella group of eleven diverse neighborhoods, created a twenty-year comprehensive plan for social, economic, and physical revitalization. The plan's desired outcomes were straightforward:

• Economic development: reduce unemployment to the city's average in five years, to the state average in ten years; create economically viable commercial districts; reduce vacant industrial space by 25 percent in five years and 50 percent in ten years.

• Education: improve student scores on standardized tests; all third graders to read at third-grade level; increase family, student, business, and community participation in schools, leading to higher school retention; use school facilities beyond traditional school hours; provide educational opportunities for dropouts and individuals over eighteen; full inclusion of students with disabilities.

• Health: universal screening, prevention, and immunization by 2001; universal health care coverage by 2018; addiction treatment on demand by 2005; drug addiction rate lowered to the national average by 2018; optimal mental health for all by 2018.

• Physical planning: reduce housing density to a sustainable level; improve physical appearance to enhance marketability; establish family-friendly neighborhood identity; raise homeownership rate to 51 percent in five years, 75 percent in twenty years; ensure open spaces are controlled and well maintained; eliminate environmental hazards by 2018; create neighborhood-friendly traffic patterns.

• Public safety: total crime rate to be reduced by 25 percent within five years, 50 percent within ten years.

• Seniors and youths: abundant opportunities for recreation and education for seniors; regular and positive interaction between youths and seniors; all young people supported and given skills to be leaders; teenage pregnancy lowered to the city average in five years, the state average in ten years; religious institutions integrated into community activities.[10]

BNIA's planned dialogue about citywide indicators is a forum for community involvement in CitiStat's development of performance metrics. It is clear that at least some of the participants have done a great deal of thinking about what's important to the health of their neighborhoods, and therefore of the city. In addition, community-based partners can give city policy makers what NASA remote-sensing specialists call "ground truth," the reality check on abstract numbers and agency claims of success.

Conclusion

Though their core missions cause one to be internally focused and the other externally, for both CitiStat and BNIA information developed from timely data is the key to community improvement (Figure 1). It is not the information itself, however, that has power. It is the technology-enhanced communication among the people generating and using information that enables them to work together more effectively to improve governance.

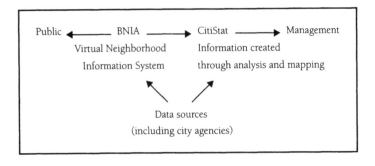

Notes

1. Grogan, P. S., and Proscio, T. *Comeback Cities.* Boulder: Westview Press, 2000, pp. 65–101.

2. www.baltimorecity.gov/neighborhoods/neighbstrat.

3. Kingsley, G. T. "Neighborhood Indicators: Taking Advantage of the New Potential." (Working paper.) Chicago: American Planning Association, Oct. 1998.

4. www.baltimorecity.gov/business/index.html, multiple dates.

5. An initiative of the Family League of Baltimore.

6. Epstein, P., Wray, L., Marshall, M., and Grifel, S. "Engaging Citizens in Achieving Results That Matter: A Model for Effective 21st Century Governance." Paper for ASPA CAP's Symposium on Results-Oriented Government, February 2000. (www.citizensleague.net/cl/SLOAN/cover.htm)

7. Urban Institute Center for Public Finance and Housing. "Democratizing Information: First Year Report of the National Neighborhood Indicators Project." Washington, D.C.: Urban Institute, Mar. 1996, pp. 48-49.

8. Urban Institute Center for Public Finance and Housing (1996), p. 47.

9. Kingsley, G. T., McNeely, J. B., and Gibson, J. O. "Community Building Coming of Age." Washington, D.C.: Development Training Institute and Urban Institute, Apr. 1997, p. 7.

10. Operation Reach Out Southwest. "Vision, Outcomes, Strategies, 1998."

Marsha R. B. Schachtel is a senior fellow at the Johns Hopkins Institute for Policy Studies.

Unraveling the Community Genome: What Makes Civil Society Work?

Suzanne W. Morse

One of the most remarkable scientific achievements of the last century was the mapping of the human genome. Since the pioneering work by Watson and Crick in deciphering the structure of DNA, scientists have made continuous progress in analyzing our genetic code. An incredible breakthrough came with the assembly of draft sequences of the approximately three billion bases making up the human genome. Now scientists have a blueprint to guide their efforts in determining the building blocks that form a human being. There is still an immense amount of work to be done, but knowledge of the human genome will lead to unparalleled advances in our understanding of medicine, disease, and biology and in our ability to improve human well-being.

In a certain sense, the task confronting communities in the twenty-first century is analogous to the effort to decode the human genome. The human genome project was a massive undertaking that required constant pursuit of scientific research in a range of areas. Thousands of people played starring roles (and some played cameos) in the drama. This same kind of painstaking and inclusive process is needed to map the foundations of a healthy and well-functioning community. Over the last decade, increasing attention has focused on determining the constituent elements of social capital, civil society, and civic engagement, which together contribute to a strong community.

However, to date much of the thinking and research on these subjects has been too narrow. Almost half a century ago, Warren Weaver listed three stages of development in the history of scientific thought.[1] First, there is the ability to deal with problems of *simplicity*. Second comes the ability to deal with problems of *disorganized complexity*. Finally, there is the ability to deal with problems of *organized complexity*. These stages create a helpful schema for advancing our thinking on civil society and the measurement of civic engagement.

We are stuck in the first stage. To move the conversation and understanding of civic engagement and civic connectedness forward, we must advance to the next stages of thought.

Measuring civil society is not a mathematical process. Civil society involves both qualitative and quantitative activities and attributes—and therein lies the rub. We have undersold the qualitative and oversold the quantitative dimensions of civil society. We are enmeshed in a web of numbers and statistics; we lack a clear picture of the whole environment. In other words, we have isolated a few civic "genes" without knowing what the complete "genome" looks like and how the various parts work together. One of the surprise discoveries from the genome project was that humans have many fewer genes than was originally thought. In fact, we have only about fifteen thousand genes more than the roundworm, and we probably have a number roughly equivalent to that of other mammals. In other words, counting alone is not enough to account for what makes a difference.

Civil society has been put under the proverbial microscope in recent years. The democratization process in Eastern Europe and the former Soviet Union was a backdrop for self-examination in America as well. However, we began to see inklings of this trend as early as 1961, with the release of Jane Jacobs's landmark book *The Death and Life of Great American Cities*. Jacobs contended that our perceived progress—the move to suburbia—was not without cost. Her picture of neighborhood life, in New York City in particular, illuminated a society in which as a matter of course individuals looked out for one another. Although her argument was primarily with planners and developers and how they design cities, the subtler message was that we were losing what makes a community work. Her words suggest an important lesson for mapping the community genome: "I shall be writing about how cities work in real life, because this is the only way to learn what principles of planning and what practices in rebuilding can promote social and economic vitality in cities, and what practices and principles will deaden their attributes."[2] Actual practice and real experience must be the primary focus for analyzing civil society.

The debate about whether our community life is better or worse than that of our parents was recently energized by the research of Robert Putnam of Harvard University. He brought renewed attention to the state of American civic life by detailing the decline in participation in traditional forms of civic engagement over the years. His title of an article and then a book, *Bowling Alone*, reflecting the decline in bowling league membership, has become a catchword in this debate. However, a recent national survey commissioned by the Pew Partnership for Civic Change and conducted by the Campaign Study Group, posed a different picture of American civic life.[3] The survey, "Ready, Willing, and Able," measured the civic connectedness of Americans, their concerns, and the kinds of individuals they identified as problem solvers.

The results contradicted the conventional picture of civic decline in that almost 80 percent of those surveyed said that they felt very connected or fairly connected to their local community. These high marks for community connectedness crossed all races, ages, and incomes. Sixty-five percent of those surveyed felt optimistic about the future of their community. Even among respondents at the lowest income level, more than half felt optimistic about the future. This response suggests that, contrary to the bowling-alone perspective that social ties are unraveling, Americans may not be as disconnected from each other as was originally thought.

The expression of connectedness and optimism reported in the survey was linked with the kinds of activity that we associate with a strong civil society: donation to charity, attendance at a religious institution, and volunteerism. Other measures painted an even clearer picture of our civil society. Seventy-seven percent of citizens surveyed said they had helped a neighbor with a problem in the preceding year. Further, 40 percent said they had gotten together with coworkers to sponsor a community activity during that same year.

However, the survey results did confirm declining trends regarding formal participation. Political activity among respondents of all ages was low. Only 12 percent said they had been active in a club or organization that deals with local government and politics, including local political campaigns. Only one-third of the respondents said they had attended a meeting of a civic organization in the last year, down from two-thirds in 1970. Perhaps the most surprising finding was that Americans aged sixty-five and older were no more likely to attend a civic-group meeting than were their fellow citizens aged twenty-nine or younger. In other words, the shift in traditional civic involvement and activities has affected the World War II generation as well as Generation X.

It seems clear that certain traditional measures of civic engagement are declining, but the question raised by the "Ready, Willing, and Able" survey is whether these are the right measures by which to assess the health of our contemporary civil society. Would we be better off if working mothers and fathers spent their evenings at a civic club meeting and participating in a bowling league? It is quite possible that in trying to map the community genome, we have not been asking the right questions or measuring the right things. If the results of this national survey are right, then maybe our benchmark should not be the activities of our parents or grandparents. Instead, we need to focus on what makes a community work *today.*

Mapping the Community Genome

Not unlike mapping the human genome, mapping the community genome requires research, observation, and understanding of the relationships between the component parts. We can identify ten elements, if not more, of a successful community:

1. Politics
2. Leadership
3. Recreation
4. Access

5. Knowledge
6. Civic participation
7. Neighborliness
8. Religion
9. Partnerships
10. Equality

This list of building blocks for successful communities challenges how we assess and measure civic engagement. In discussing each element below, I highlight a key question for future deliberation.

Politics. Voting trends since 1960 indicate a steady decline in overall voter turnout. But as we look at the most recent presidential election, we see that more African Americans voted than in 1960 (as was also true for women), and that more people voted overall in 2000 than in 1960—approximately one-half of the two hundred million or so registered voters cast their ballots in November 2000. This number is large enough to indicate more than a passing interest by the public in the last election, but it is clear that a large number of registered voters chose not to participate. The next four years will be brimming with proposals and efforts to reform the voting process—the methods, the machines, and the mechanics.

According to "Ready, Willing, and Able," 57 percent of Americans still feel that voting makes a difference on how decisions are made, yet a number of those people stayed home. Why? There are some real structural barriers to voting; time, place, and access are only a few. Voting percentages will only get stronger if voting and other forms of direct participation show a clear correlation with action and policy and if issues, not money, drive campaigns. From the results of this survey, the most promising place to start these reforms is at the local level. One of the most compelling questions we must answer in this regard is how elected officials can effectively engage citizens in the policy process to restore trust and involvement.

Leadership. Every community has a few key people to whom its citizens turn for answers. Sometimes they are elected officials, sometimes local business people. This model worked well when people thought solutions were simple and were willing to allow the few to decide for the many. The lack of progress in social issues over the last few decades has called attention to the inability of any group, no matter how savvy, to speak on behalf of all citizens. New approaches to leadership require that the community look broadly and deeply for community and neighborhood leaders. No longer can the corporate model of leadership training be enough. We must build a critical mass of citizens who work on behalf of the community and who represent it. This process involves new thinking, new ways of identifying leaders, and new models of training. The question for this second element of a successful community is, Who do we need to solve the problem?

Recreation. Public spaces for recreation can connect or divide a community. If opponents want to thwart integration, they shut down the parks and swimming pools. A successful community has places where strangers can mingle and interact. Jacobs described the street in front of her brownstone in New York as teeming with people who watched out for one another. The early planners of Minneapolis created a park within every six blocks. Communities from Peoria to Philadelphia understand the galvanizing role that a sports team can play in a community. Citywide youth sports, walking trails at parks and in shopping malls, and adult softball leagues bring together strangers as well as friends. The compelling question is not how many people play but how pervasive and accessible public recreation is to the entire community.

Access. Access to transportation is critical. Certainly the mobility that comes with public transportation is important. Access to the community, however, has a larger focus: the opportunity to get to know the community. Technology has helped the process through such means as community bulletin boards and Web pages, but we know that these bypass a large segment of the population. Multiple venues, repetition, and notices in various languages are required to provide sufficient access to information about community events.

The real test of community access, though, is not how successful we are in distributing information but whether we are creating places and opportunities in neighborhoods, cities, and rural areas for people to get to know each other. If you must board a bus to shop for groceries, you are unlikely to see your fellow shoppers strolling down your neighborhood street. If you work nights and sleep days, you may not have the opportunity to visit your child's school at a time when other parents are there. If you work two jobs, it is unlikely you will have much time to grill in the backyard or talk with neighbors. Fear and distrust are real, but another reality of modern-day life is the lack of opportunity for even casual interaction. The question to be answered for this element is one that Jacobs might have asked: How can we build and facilitate communities that foster interaction and access to one another?

Knowledge. Information has always been, and always will be, a powerful weapon against ignorance, bigotry, and authoritarianism. In the early days of our country, Thomas Jefferson spoke of the need for an informed citizenry. As we create a society that is better connected, it is critical that we reactivate avenues of community knowledge. This cannot be done solely through technology, although our opportunities for outreach have increased with technology. Nor can we delegate responsibility for providing knowledge about the community's issues to the local media.

Although the information age has given us more options for traditional and nontraditional media, communities must be proactive about providing mechanisms for citizens to discuss issues and exchange information—virtually and visually. Citizens are often overwhelmed by a glut of conflicting positions. On everything from taxes to childcare, we encounter conflicting "expert" opinions. This is particularly true around election or referendum time. Community media as well as citizens' organizations can offer information in nonpartisan, nonconfrontational ways. Issues can be discussed, debated, and understood to allow choice and action. The question for this fifth element of a successful community is whether we have enough opportunities for citizens to discuss the issues and make informed decisions on the matters that affect them the most.

Civic Participation. Community support for local causes is about more than hours spent or money given. At the end of the day, it is about tuning into the needs of the community. We must think strategically and creatively about how to promote citizen engagement that gets at the root of problems and their solutions. This requires that we reconfigure our old notions of support for local causes and volunteerism generally. In the final analysis, support for community organizations and issues must have as a primary goal building a constituency for change. It is no longer feasible to ask citizens to give of their time or their money as charity alone. We must have demonstrable results, a plan for sustainability, and a vision of the big picture. The larger question for civic participation is how donating time and money can galvanize the community to invest and support efforts that are sustainable and that work over time.

Neighborliness. People connect to other people and to places. At the most basic level, community is about where and with whom you live. Neighborliness comes as much from friendly people as from circumstances that allow and support the interaction of people. Amid the busyness of contemporary life, it is critical to afford opportunities for people who live in traditional neighborhoods, high-rise apartments, or even gated communities to interact with one another. The first step in this process must be to ensure a safe environment. We can't force people to be friendly and outgoing, but we can create an atmosphere of community security that encourages the natural instinct of human beings: to connect with each other. We need to know more about how to create a community of interaction.

Religion. Affiliation with a formal religious organization fosters connection to community. Beyond the personal spiritual journey, communities benefit from people who are connected to others in a community of faith. In the "Ready, Willing, and Able" survey, among those who reported feeling most connected to their communities 60 percent said they regularly attend religious services. A similar number said that local churches, synagogues, and mosques are important or crucial to finding solutions to community problems. Religious affiliation is about stepping outside yourself, being accountable, and being in community. These attributes apply to community life as well. The question for this eighth community element is how religious organizations can be an inclusive vehicle for community building.

Partnerships. A majority of Americans would agree that community problems are too big for any individual to solve them alone. However, our ability to bridge sectoral lines to define, diagnose, or solve community problems remains inadequate. Fewer than two-thirds of Americans feel their local officials work well together, yet the systemic problems facing all communities affect government, business, and the nonprofit sector. Creating opportunity for community organizations from all sectors to work together and to carve out particular areas of expertise is the only way that progress will be made on the critical issues of the day. We need to nurture and develop ways to encourage and structure community partnerships to get better results for the whole community.

Equality. Acceptance and recognition of others begins with equal treatment and respect. Civil society does not work if we divide and separate ourselves by class, race, economic status, or any other of a whole range of "isms." Common dreams, shared visions, and a sense of fairness and equity join people. Philosopher Hannah Arendt contended that citizens must have the skills, and the space, to come together to discuss and decide critical community issues; in effect, they must meet as equals to deal with issues of common concern.[4] The question for this final community component is, How can we better provide opportunities for citizens in the community to meet as equals in deciding the critical issues of the day?

What Constitutes the Health of Our Civic Life?

Questions concerning the health of our civic life have stimulated rich and productive discussions among organizations and individuals seeking to diagnose and remedy our civic malaise. Sometimes, however, it seems that our perception of society gets worse the more we examine it. It is essential to consider our present circumstances in light of both past trends and changes from past conditions.

After World War II, the world changed in a number of important ways. Veterans returned to work, tract homes and suburban neighborhoods burgeoned, and progress was made in civil rights for minorities and women. The Cleavers were home . . . or were they? We have painted a picture of the forties and fifties that reflects a civic utopia. This view of the world in the decades following World War II, however, is deceptive. Segregation was alive and well; women and minorities were paid more poorly and were offered less meaningful work than white men; and the level of poverty approached 25 percent of the population. Yet in 1960, a record number of registered voters voted. We had more women and men participating in civic organizations, and we had a sense that our streets were safer. It was civic schizophrenia.

As we consider our own civic life, it is important to keep the benchmarks of civic engagement current so that they accurately reflect the kind of society we want and require. The view looking backward suggests a higher degree of social connectedness then. Whether apocryphal or not, the conventional view is that our parents knew their neighbors better than we do. Our fathers ran with the Elks and the Lions more regularly. The Eastern Star, the League of Women Voters, and the local women's auxiliary were thriving.

Then things changed. Women went to work in record numbers. Families moved away from the center city. With the pressures of work, parents began to cut down on outside activity. The civil rights movement gathered strength, and important legal victories were won, dismantling segregation. The Vietnam War and Watergate tore the nation apart both at home and abroad. Eighteen-year-olds were given the right to vote.

There was definitely a shift over this period in how Americans spent their time, how they viewed the nation's place in the world, and how they defined equality for all. Herein lies a quandary for defining and analyzing American civil society. Our benchmarks for judging today's civil society may not be commensurate with standards that were used before. We should retain some of these measures, but perhaps not all of them. We should not reminisce about the things that have been lost without recognizing the things that our society has gained. This understanding calls for a new conversation and debate about the composition of our civic life and what makes it work.

The bowling metaphor has been effective in putting the issue of our civic health in local terms. As people ride down the street, they see bowling lanes that have closed down; the metaphor rings true. But in our proverbial cruise down Main Street, we see some things that we didn't see when bowling was at its peak. There are soccer fields galore, complete with parent coaches, cheering relatives, and local referees. Further down the street, you are likely to see a health club or two and a public outdoor running track.

Go to any community in America, and you will find a festival or celebration that is inclusive and celebratory of the community's uniqueness. Waynesville, Ohio, is famous for its Sauerkraut Festival, as is Bakersville, North Carolina, for its Rhododendron Festival. If we took all the Dogwood Parades, Cinco de Mayo Festivals, Juneteenth celebrations, Veteran's Day, fire company and St. Patrick's Day parades, and the whole host of seasonal and religious observances, we could fill up our calendars many times over. When asked to describe their own community life, many citizens do not accept the notion that they are not connected to each other in their own community. Most people express misgivings about our shared political life, but they are not reticent in describing their positive connection to their community.

What Can We Do Better?

Despite the fact that in general Americans feel good about where they live, the "Ready, Willing, and Able" survey revealed some serious concerns. When asked what the major problems in their community are, citizens listed lack of jobs that pay a living wage, unavailability of affordable health care, and use and distribution of illegal drugs. Although not civic issues in the strictest sense, these responses speak volumes about the quality of our shared community lives. It is generally agreed that we have experienced a breakdown in American family life. One of the culprits is surely the fact that parents must work two or more jobs to make ends meet.

Skeptics might contend that our consumer wants exceed our ability to pay. Surely overspending and "overwanting" cause some families to work two or more jobs, but living-wage jobs are not about luxury; rather, they are meant to ensure the essentials of food, decent shelter, and clothing to a family. According to national statistics, many families cannot make ends meet between a minimum wage whose value has not kept pace with inflation and the relatively high cost of basic necessities. According to a report from the National Low Income Housing Coalition, full-time minimum-wage workers cannot afford the fair market rent (FMR) for a one-bedroom apartment, as determined by the U.S. Housing and Urban Development agency. Furthermore, in seventy metropolitan areas, minimum-wage workers would have to work more than one hundred hours a week to afford FMR.[5] Twenty percent of Americans who live in poverty are employed. The first step in improving our civil society is to level the playing field. How can we expect citizens to engage in a system that does not work for them?

The survey respondents indicated that health care was the second major concern. They didn't say health care for just themselves or their families; they said health care for everyone. How does health care relate to civic life? There are two answers. First, affordable health care levels the playing field. It assures an individual of the ability to have physical well-being as an affordable priority, it allows children to have the timely care they need, and it stretches a family's income further. Second, although good health is not an inalienable right in the strictest sense, it is a building block for making our communities healthier and fairer. We must address the issue of health care and public health in the context of our community life.

The third major area of concern was the use and distribution of illegal drugs. Certainly, respondents want drugs off the street, but their concerns are also related to community life generally. This concern has much to do with neighborhood safety and the well-being of young people. Citizens feel that drug use and related crime and disruption keep them captive in their homes and create an environment in which young people are particularly vulnerable. Civil society at its core depends on trust and interaction. In many neighborhoods that once thrived, the presence of illegal drugs has drained the civic spirit from the lifeblood of the community. According to the *KIDS COUNT Data Book, 2000*, "the reality and perception of danger clearly have an impact on whether and how families in poor communities spend time together or with their neighbors. Families are reluctant to gather in parks or playgrounds or venture out after dark with their kids. Grandparents and other older residents—who have much to offer and much to gain from family and community networks—often remain homebound, not because they are ill or frail, but out of fear for their safety."[6]

Safety is an essential prerequisite for a flourishing civil society, as are living-wage jobs and a healthy populace. The quality of civic participation cannot be assessed in isolation from the fundamental obligation to meet basic human needs.

There are probably hundreds of factors that have influenced the changes in our civil society since World War II. Observers who point to television viewing, women entering the (paid) workforce in greater numbers, or even the advent of air conditioning as factors all make a plausible case. We have come off the front porch, turned on the tube, and rested our bodies from the day's work. Most people, it is true, are not talking over the backyard fence as they hang the day's wash; nor is there a time set aside in the rhythms of community life in which everybody is in the same place. In an era when almost every retail store is open on Sunday, we have lost the time and the opportunity for much of the visiting of yesterday. The magnetic poles of community life are working against each other, one pulling for more work and the other pulling for more quality time and involvement with family, neighbors, and even strangers.

This point came through in the "Ready, Willing, and Able" survey. When asked if they get involved enough in efforts to improve the community, 70 percent said they do not. Yet in interviews with citizens who had not volunteered in the last year, more than 40 percent said they would volunteer if they knew how to go about it or whom to call. Further, 60 percent said they would volunteer if they had more time. The number who volunteer ebbs and flows, but it appears that Americans are ready, willing, and able to do more.

Conclusion

We do not have a sufficient understanding of why civil society is what it is today. Nor do we have a firm, shared sense of what we want it to be. We think we have some reliable clues, but civil society is as complicated to dissect as the human body. Too much of the national conversation centers on voting and visible participation. These forms of participation are a critical bellwether, but we must branch out, think creatively, and observe less obvious forms of participation and the patterns of engagement that now exist.

A number of years ago, I was asked by a newspaper reporter to comment on the state of civil society. I could only repeat what I had read and heard as fact, that things weren't so great. The conversation didn't open up until I began to reflect on what I had seen in two decades of public policy work. Yes, the public is disillusioned with Washington and the big business of national politics. Yes, the era of mergers, cutbacks, and huge corporate salaries has turned people off and eroded confidence. But no, I did not see distrustful or inactive communities. Quite the contrary, ten years of research in and with fifty cities speaks volumes about what we aren't talking about—what we don't know. Former Senator and presidential aspirant Bill Bradley uses the metaphor of society as a three-legged stool, supported by civil society, the public sector, and the private sector. The civil society leg has perhaps been analyzed with too much attention to quantitative factors. If we want to rebuild and strengthen our civil society, we need to do what the genome researchers did: build on what we know, discover what we don't know, and document the results.

Civil society in America is not perfect. At the same time, the country is brimming with the hope and possibility that have eluded demographers, statisticians, and historians. The ten elements in the community map listed here point to different directions for community work. They remind us to be cautious not to apply old standards to new possibilities. The community genome is just beginning to be mapped and understood. It will take more research, more listening, and more reflection to fully understand the potential avenues for increasing civic engagement and improving our shared lives. But as St. Francis of Assisi reminded us, you start by doing what is necessary; then you do what is possible; and suddenly you are doing the impossible.

Notes

1. Cited in Jacobs, J. *The Death and Life of Great American Cities.* New York: Vintage, 1961.
2. Jacobs (1961), p. 4.
3. "Ready, Willing, and Able." Charlottesville, Va.: Pew Partnership for Civic Change, 2001.
4. Bernstein, R. J. 1986. *Religion in American Public Life.* Mahwah, N.J.: Paulist Press.
5. "Out of Reach: The Gap Between Housing Costs and Income of Poor People in the United States." Washington, DC.: National Low Income Housing Coalition, 1999.
6. *KIDS COUNT Data Book 2000.* Baltimore: Annie E. Casey Foundation, 2000, p. 12.

Suzanne W. Morse is the executive director of the Pew Center for Civic Change.

Collaboration Through Network Structures for Community Building Efforts

Myrna P. Mandell

Public policy makers are looking for innovative solutions to complex social, economic, and environmental problems that are beyond the capacity of any one group or organization to solve. Governments are experimenting with developing equal partnerships involving communities, nongovernmental organizations, and the private sector.[1] Such a collaboration can be called a network or network structure.[2] Study of collaboration of this type is changing our traditional view of what is meant by governance and the role of nongovernmental groups and organizations in solving complex public problems.

In the area of community development, for instance, we recognize that community problems (regarding health, economic development, crime) do not come in nice, neat bundles. Although there may be a number of groups or organizations that deal with particular facets of them, these problems are complex and cannot be easily handled by any one group or organization. Instead, they can only be managed through collaborative effort.[3] Network structures have therefore been used to encourage community involvement and innovative solution of complex problems.

Unfortunately, public administrators are often poorly equipped to deal with the challenges inherent in dealing with the gamut of nongovernmental organizations, community groups, and businesses involved in this unique type of program operation.[4] As a result, although collaboration is often seen as the panacea for these problems, establishing a network structure has not always resulted in the most effective outcome. Part of the problem is that network structures are not well understood, particularly when it comes to managing conflict; dealing with issues of power, influence, and control; developing new modes of leadership; and building trust.

Understanding Types of Collaboration

Because they are on the front line in dealing with today's complex social problems, public administrators as well as local communities need to know how to get the most out of a collaborative effort. Here are three important issues to consider in this regard:

1. Differences between private sector and public sector network structures
2. Not only understanding the opportunities and promises of collaboration but also dealing with the pitfalls and constraints surrounding collaboration of various types
3. The need to develop a revised perspective of management and the strategies needed in network structures[5]

The concepts of network and network structure are at the forefront of a move to develop innovative ways to design programs and build stronger communities. The need for a manager, whether in the public or the private sector, to understand how to manage collaboration is therefore a major concern for the future. Researchers and practitioners use such labels as *partnership, network,* and *collaboration* interchangeably, ignoring the fact that these institutions differ along many variables, among them relative stability, degree of interdependence, and number of organizations involved in the effort.[6]

Collaboration can be seen as occupying a continuum, from loosely formed partnerships with a narrow focus and great independence (such as a contractual relationship or a task force) to more structured and interdependent collaboration encompassing broad systems change to accomplish a common policy goal (as with a network structure). All of these innovations differ from traditional organizational structures by having a more participatory and nonhierarchical orientation.

The major difference among the types of network is the degree to which the individual member (that is, organizational unit) remains separate and autonomous or forms a new, combined unit for long-term change and interaction. Networks at one end of the continuum tend to be marked by some combination of these features:

- The member organizations exhibit loose linkage and have limited commitment to each other
- There may be simultaneous or coordinated action among the various members, but each acts as an independently operating organization
- The member organization anticipates relatively little change in its normal operations

Networks clustered at the opposite end of this idealized spectrum also claim particular features:

- There is tight linkage and a strong commitment to the whole among the individual member organizations
- There is a high degree of risk for the member organization
- The organization is expected to be committed to major systems change

Although the function that the collaborative structure is intended to accomplish can guide the choice of what type of network to use, knowing how to manage effectively within the collaborative structure is the key. Actions that may be effective for contractual alignment are not effective for a network structure. Instead of blaming the collaboration in and of itself for an ineffective policy solution, what is needed is an understanding of how to make the collaboration work in the first place.

Network Structure

In a number of studies on community-building efforts,[7] it has been found that the most effective efforts are based on formation of a network structure, which "consists of public, private, not-for-profit organizations and community groups in an active, organized collaboration to accomplish some agreed upon purpose or purposes. Network structures may require separate actions on the part of the individual members, but the participants are transformed into a new whole, taking on broad tasks that reach beyond the simultaneous actions of independently operating organizations. Network structures may include, but go beyond, informal linkages, co-ordination, task force action or coalitional activity."[8]

A network structure is distinguished from traditional organizational structures because there is no one "in charge."[9] This does not necessarily mean there is no lead agency or foundation setting up the formal rules of the collaboration. But it is the case that typical forms of power and authority do not work in a network structure. Although some actors may have more formal power (in terms of resources or political clout) than others, this power cannot be used to unilateral effect unilaterally since each member is an independent entity. In addition, informal power based on interpersonal relations can be more important than formal power. This means that new modes of leadership featuring "facilitators" or "brokers" may be used.

Rather than relying on contractual arrangements (although there may be some contracts as part of the collaboration), a network structure relies on exchange based on interpersonal relations. This means that to be effective, managers must be able to trust one another to work to everyone's mutual benefit. This trust may not be easy to build in the political arena. However, there are two other aspects of a network structure that can be successfully used to deal with this problem.

First, forming a network structure means at least some of the members recognize that their purposes cannot be achieved independently and thus all action is mutually interdependent. Second, many of the participants may already know each other and have formed "pockets of trust" among themselves prior to forming the network structure. Participants can capitalize on these pockets of trust by using effective management strategies.

The strength of a network structure, therefore, depends significantly on the degree to which the members understand and can take advantage of these fundamental realities. The members must recognize the pitfalls and the opportunities presented in forming the network structure, and they must be able to apply effective management techniques to handle the constraints.

Difference Between Networks in the Public and Private Sectors

Public policy makers and managers in public administration operate under a set of circumstances that differ significantly from those in the private sector. Collaboration through networks is a feature of both sectors, but in the private sector it is often characterized by partnership and alliance, meant to benefit a particular company or industry. Conversely, collaboration through networks in the public sector involves disparate organizations working toward a common goal, not merely to enhance the performance of one organization among them. This has been referred to as the difference between vertical and horizontal management.[10] Therefore, much of the work on collaboration through networks that has been published in the business management literature does not apply wholesale and without revision to the public sector.

A number of authors[11] have emphasized the importance of understanding that management in a network structure is different from management in a traditional organization. These authors have suggested a number of approaches to understanding these management strategies and how they relate specifically to collaboration through network structure.

Understanding the Complexity of Managing a Network

In a recent paper, Mandell and Steelman[12] present a synthesis of the managerial strategies that apply to a network structure. They are classified according to the ability to (1) influence members to participate, (2) secure commitment from members, and (3) create a favorable environment for productive interaction.

Influencing members to participate refers to two behaviors. The first has to do with the need to secure the support of participants who can sustain and build legitimacy for the network. There is a difference between participants who invest energy in the work to be done in the network (champions) and those who have the ability to legitimize the network through persuasion and influence (sponsors).[13] Both are needed in a network structure. Agranoff and McGuire[14] refer to the ability to tap into the skills, knowledge, and resources needed to sustain a network structure as "activation." Complementing this skill is an equally important strategy, "de-activation," which involves introducing new actors to change network dynamics when appropriate.[15]

The second behavior in influencing members to participate refers to rules, procedures, values, and norms. This has to do with altering the perception of the network participant, which includes framing, or the ability to influence prevailing values and norms; developing a shared purpose or program rationale; and developing a vision to focus attention on synergistic purposes.[16]

The second of the three abilities, securing commitment from members, refers to getting the participants to take joint action. Agranoff and McGuire[17] refer to this as the "power to" bring about cooperation rather than the "power over" others. It involves developing cooperation and collaboration among a diverse group that might not ordinarily cooperate with each other. Accomplishing this requires the strategies of mobilization behavior to marshal resources, build a coalition, and forge agreements[18]; and developing a view of the whole to achieve a set of common objectives.[19]

The third strategic ability, creating a favorable environment for productive interaction, refers to minimizing the costs to the participant. It has been referred to as synthesizing or arranging[20] the network. It involves building management skills in which the role of a manager is changed from being "in charge" to being a multilateral broker or facilitator.[21] These skills include the ability to blend many cultures, needs, and goals to facilitate interaction among participants; secure a working consensus on behalf of the whole, while allowing participants to contribute for their own reasons; and develop effective communication among participants.

The Impact of Management Strategy on Community Collaboration

As pointed out by Agranoff and McGuire, multiple behaviors are used in networks, and often they overlap. For instance, "after or during deactivation or reframing, managers must mobilize support for the changes, reestablish the purpose of the network, and make sure all participants are 'on board.'"[22] Good communication skills and the ability to build areas of trust are essential to forming an effective network.

The abiding situational complexity that attends any network structure ensures that the manager must be aware that noble goals and best intentions may be thwarted. Before forming any type of network, therefore, managers must be cognizant of the constraints and opportunities present within their own situation and make the best use of these factors. Where conditions are favorable, the manager may find that the difficulties encountered in even the most complex type of network can be alleviated to a great extent through the foundation already built on informal relationships.

Community Collaboration in the Case of New Futures

This case study, focusing on a program called New Futures (NF), indicates the difficulty of achieving effective outcomes in light of situational realities. In this instance, effective strategies, coupled with recognition of the constraints and opportunities present in the particular situation, led to limited success. In the end, however, situational difficulties frustrated the collaboration and the network structure eventually dissolved.

NF was a program developed through individual grants from the Annie E. Casey Foundation. The program was initiated in a number of cities across the United States in the middle and late 1980s. This analysis focuses on the program implemented in Dayton, Ohio. The program was designed to "adjust systems—schools, health, human services agencies, criminal justice, and other major actors—to produce more favorable outcomes for young people."[23] This broad mission elicited commitment among participants to take joint and strategically interdependent action to realize overriding goals on behalf of the entire community. The collaboration that was developed meets the definition of a network structure.

The major thrust of the program was preventing truancy. The foundation gave the lead role to the school superintendent on behalf of the school system. The initial activities of the program focused on efforts that would directly enhance attendance by the targeted students.

The city of Dayton has a great deal of experience in developing problem-solving networks. By the time the NF grant was written, the city was committed to working on behalf of the total community, and it ensured that as many community members (including youths) were included as possible (*developing a vision*). City officials also made sure that a number of key participants who each had a reputation for working on behalf of the city and who had the ability to influence others to commit resources to this type of effort were invited to the table (*securing champions and sponsors*).

The member organizations and participants were:

Dayton Public Schools
Department of Human Services (public welfare)
Montgomery County Children Services (child welfare)
Miami Valley Child Development Centers (Head Start)
Montgomery County Juvenile Court
The mental health board
The Combined (city-county) Health District
City of Dayton, City Manager's Office
Montgomery County, Community Human Services Department
Miami Valley Hospital
University of Dayton
Sinclair Community College
United Way
Ohio Governor's Office
Township Trustees
Business and labor representatives
Civic associations
Dayton's neighborhood Priority Boards
Citizen activists

It was not long before a critical core of the participants began to reshape efforts to follow the guidelines, to meet what they perceived was the real reason for initiating the network (*framing; developing a program rationale*). These participants represented all of the public sector agencies. They even invited the school superintendent to join them, but he refused because his perception was that he was "in charge." They set up regular meetings in which they built on previous relationships and forged stronger pockets of trust and relations in which to take action (*mobilization behavior*). Through their actions, they were able to secure commitment to take broader action on behalf of children and families as a whole throughout the community (*synthesizing and arranging; developing a view of the whole*). They also undertook a second wave of activity to expand the reach of the program beyond school instruction by including other child and youth service agencies. These activist participants developed a series of interagency agreements (*mobilization behavior*) that went beyond the requirements of the initial grant.

When these participants in the network redefined their purpose to include the welfare of children and families in the community as a whole (*securing a working consensus on behalf of the whole*), the school superintendent's ability to continue on his narrow course of action was jeopardized. The other members recognized the need to come together in new ways that would require a commitment to systems change throughout their community (*developing a view of the whole*), but the school superintendent continued to use the grant only for school services. Once these two definitions of the issue collided, the effectiveness of the collaboration was in jeopardy.

The formal rules set up by the foundation gave the superintendent the power to resist actions suggested by other participants in the network. The informal rules established by these other actors allowed them to build a power base with which to oppose the school superintendent's position, thus permitting far-reaching actions to be taken. Yet the other participants in NF were not able to secure the superintendent's support for these actions (*creating a favorable environment for productive interaction*), and the foundation did not renew the grant.

Lessons Learned

This case points to a number of lessons concerning the impact of contextual variables on the effectiveness of a given management strategy in a network structure. The school superintendent interpreted the rules of the supporting foundation according to his own perceptions and needs. How the rules were written (making the schools the lead agency) permitted him to do so. But the past history of relations among other city agencies and participating organizations provided a means for these organizations to challenge the superintendent's ability to implement the foundation's rules.

This opposition eventually led the foundation to reevaluate the effect that its rules had on how network structures pursue systemic change. It also made the city more aware of the impact that one person or organization could have on the effectiveness of a network and indicated once again the difficulty of implementing even the most well-meaning community effort.

Although a network structure relies on horizontal collaborative efforts, this does not mean that traditional hierarchical relationships disappear. The formal rules that a foundation or government agency puts into place to guide how its resources are used creates a position of power for the organizations in the network structure that is established. To the extent that the foundation or lead agency is setting up a network structure to foster a collaborative solution, however, its reliance on traditional (hierarchical) managerial techniques must be tempered by a need to allow more flexible horizontal relations. This was the lesson that the Annie E. Casey Foundation had to learn the hard way in the case of NF.

Finally, network structures are not set up to deliver services. That is something individual organizations in the network structure do. Instead, the network structure is set up to allow the members to make decisions about systems reform (that is, binding decisions that cut across delivery systems). Such decisions may entail a high degree of risk for a member organization used to the status quo. Depending on the political realities of the situation, the risks may prove too great to be overcome. But if the members come together because they recognize that the prevailing arrangement has not worked and will not work, then at least there is a basis for discussing systems change. Without this recognition, setting up a network structure would seem pointless.

There are not usually any easy choices, and circumstances may lead to collaborative effort that is not quite what managers hoped for. In the end, however, this is what management through network structure is about: understanding the realities of the situation, capitalizing on the opportunities, minimizing the constraints, and working, even incrementally, toward effective joint outcomes.

Notes

1. For a synopsis of this trend, see Kickert, W.J.M., Klijn, E.-H., and Koppenjan, J.F.M. (eds.). *Managing Complex Networks: Strategies for the Public Sector.* London: Sage, 1997; and Mandell, M. P. (ed.). "The Impact of Collaborative Efforts: Changing the Face of Public Policy Through Networks and Network Structures." (Special Symposium.) *Policy Studies Review,* 1999, *16* (1), 4–147.

2. Mandell, M. P. "A Revised Look at Management in Network Structures." *International Journal of Organizational Theory and Behavior,* 2000, *3* (1 and 2), 185–210.

3. Gage, R., and Mandell, M. P. *Strategies for Managing Intergovernmental Policies and Networks.* New York: Praeger, 1990.

4. O'Toole, L., Jr. "Treating Networks Seriously: Practical and Research-Based Agendas in Public Administration." *Public Administration Review,* 1997, *57* (1), 45–52.

5. Mandell, M. P. (ed.). *Getting Results Through Collaboration: Networks and Network Structures for Public Policy and Management.* Westport, Conn.: Quorum Press, in press.

6. Cigler, B. A. "Pre-Conditions for the Emergence of Multicommunity Collaborative Organizations." *Policy Studies Review,* 1999, *16* (1), 86–102; Mandell, M. P., and Steelman, T. "Understanding What Can Be Accomplished Through Interorganizational Relationships: The Importance of Typologies, Context and Management Strategies." Unpublished manuscript.

7. Mandell (1999); Mandell (in press).

8. Mandell (1999), p. 45.

9. Mandell (1999).

10. Agranoff, R., and McGuire, M. "After the Network Is Formed: Process, Power and Performance." In M. P. Mandell (in press).

11. Agranoff and McGuire (in press); Steelman, T., and Carmin, J. "Community Based Watershed Remediation: Connecting Organizational Resources to Social and Substantive Outcomes." In D. Rahm (ed.), *The Politics of Toxic Waste: 21st Century Challenges.* McFarland Publishers, in press; and O'Toole (1997).

12. Mandell and Steelman (unpublished).

13. Mandell (in press).

14. Agranoff and McGuire (in press).

15. Agranoff and McGuire (in press).

16. Agranoff and McGuire (in press); Mandell (2000); Porter, D. O. "Accounting for Discretion and Local Environments in Social Experimentation and Program Administration: Some Proposed Alternative Conceptualizations." In K. L. Bradbury and A. Downs (eds.), *Do Housing Allowances Work?* Washington, D.C.: Brookings Institution, 1981.

17. Agranoff and McGuire (in press).

18. Agranoff and McGuire (in press); Mandell (2000).

19. Mandell, M. P. "Intergovernmental Management in Interorganizational Networks: A Revised Perspective." *International Journal of Public Administration,* 1988, *11* (4), 393–416.

20. Agranoff and McGuire (in press); Klijn, E.-H., and Teisman, G. R. "Strategies and Games in Networks." In Kickert, Klijn, and Koppenjan (1997).

21. Mandell (1988); Gray, B. *Collaborating: Finding Common Ground for Multiparty Problems.* San Francisco: Jossey-Bass, 1989.

22. Agranoff and McGuire (in press).

23. Mandell, M. P. "Managing Interdependencies Through Program Structures: A Revised Paradigm." *American Review of Public Administration,* 1994, *25* (1), 99–121.

Myrna P. Mandell is a professor of management at California State University, Northridge.

Building Better Citizens: Increasing the Level of Civic Education Among Teens in Jacksonville, Florida

Pamela Zeiser

Building Better Citizens is a program that clearly states its mission. The need to increase civic education among young people is evident from recent U.S. Department of Education reports, scholarly articles, and news media accounts chronicling low voter turnout among young adults, a distressingly low level of civic knowledge among high school seniors, and the detachment young adults demonstrate with regard to government and our governmental processes. Many civic and leadership programs focus on students who excel in their studies and have demonstrated leadership skills, but Building Better Citizens focuses on a population that is often overlooked: disadvantaged teenagers in alternative schools.

The University of North Florida's Institute of Government (an affiliate of the Florida Institute of Government at the Florida State University) and Girls Incorporated of Jacksonville (Girls, Inc.) cosponsored Building Better Citizens. The program was implemented at the PACE Center for Girls in Jacksonville, Florida, a school for young women with academic, criminal, or social problems. The teenagers in the program participated in an active and experiential learning environment that measurably increased their civic knowledge: test results demonstrated that most students improved from a grade of F to a B.

Young women attend the PACE center for many reasons, among them expulsion from a traditional school, criminal offense, abuse, and disrupted family life. These students face many challenges to obtaining an education and are rarely perceived as leaders in their communities. For many, their experience of government is limited to negative aspects of the legal and welfare systems. It was

Thank you to Sarah Monroe of the University of North Florida Institute of Government, Geneva Shanholtzer of PACE, and Kit Thomas of Girls, Inc. The Institute of Government at the University of North Florida is an affiliate of the Florida Institute of Government located at the Florida State University. The Building Better Citizens Program was funded by the Deer Creek Foundation and the Kirbo Foundation.

exciting and rewarding to have an opportunity to expose this population to government in a positive way and to empower them as citizens. One class of nineteen young women, ages fifteen through eighteen, participated in the program.

Building Better Citizens' objectives included increasing the participants' knowledge of local, state, and federal government; motivating them to become involved in community issues and needs; and building an understanding of what it means to be a responsible and involved citizen. The curriculum was both classroom-based and experiential. It informed students about the electoral process, voting, and presidential candidates; taught them about volunteering, the role of nonprofit organizations, and the value of contributing to the community; and prompted them to think about responsible citizenship. Classroom activities were lectures, presentations from local nonprofit organizations, research, a mock presidential election, and journals. Experiential activities included visiting local Democratic and Republican party headquarters, visiting City Hall, and a group volunteer activity at a local homeless shelter. The mock presidential election was one of the big successes of the project. (Former Vice President Gore won by just a few votes.) Participants became very involved in researching candidates and then campaigning for their favorite. The students even shared what they learned with the whole school, by making informational campaign posters and hanging them in the hallway outside their classroom.

Evaluation of the Building Better Citizens program included pretests and posttests to measure civic education and attitudes. Test questions asked how often elections are held, who the current governor of Florida is, the role of elected representatives, and so forth. The increase in civic knowledge gained was dramatic. The average posttest score was 76 percent, a statistically significant increase over the average pretest score of 56 percent (were grades assigned to these scores, the average grade on the pretest would have been an F and the high score a D). On the posttest, the lowest grade was a D, the average grade was B-, and the most common grade was B. This is progress any educator would be proud of, and it clearly shows the value of Building Better Citizens.

The pretest and posttest included questions to measure civic attitudes, such as whether it is important to vote, what it means to be a responsible citizen, and whether citizens can help solve community problems. Of course, changing attitudes—civic or otherwise—is a slow and difficult process. The success of Building Better Citizens was in prompting students to think about civic values and form opinions on these matters, perhaps for the first time. Far more participants responded "don't know" on the pretest (32 percent) than the posttest (7 percent) to questions about serious problems in Jacksonville and what it means to be a responsible citizen. I interpret this change to mean that participants became more aware of problems and developed personal opinions about being a responsible citizen. Answers to the civic attitude questions represent a clearly positive trend.

Participant evaluations of Building Better Citizens were very positive. Students saw value in the program, enjoyed themselves, and indicated that the program helped them become more involved citizens. Many undertook individual volunteer projects. At the beginning of the program, 16 percent of the participants said they "often" talked with family and friends about politics or community problems; at the end, this increased to 40 percent. By sharing what they learned with others, participants became involved in community issues and demonstrated an understanding of how dialogue is part of being a responsible and involved citizen. Overall, participants felt they learned about government in a fun way and expressed enthusiasm for continuation of the project.

A real strength of Building Better Citizens was that participants were treated as leaders and the curriculum cultivated leadership skills. This approach prevented students from viewing the program as remedial. This particular group of students—those who do not fit in well at a traditional educational setting—reacted quite positively to this approach and thus to the program. On the evaluations, one student noted, "I enjoyed just seeing them [the outside people conducting the program] come and them wanting to be involved with PACE girls." Many of the participants indicated their appreciation that outsiders were interested in teaching them, speaking to them, and involving them in the program's activities.

Teenagers' detachment from their community and government, generally speaking, was one of the original reasons for creating the Building Better Citizens program. The participants' gratitude—and even surprise—at being invited to participate in the program is encouraging and holds hope that, with a little effort on the part of adults and educators, teenagers can become more interested and better informed participants in our governmental system.

The Building Better Citizens program is continuing in Jacksonville and has been shared with Girls, Inc., groups throughout the southern United States. On objective and subjective measures, the program succeeded well in increasing civic knowledge and attitudes. A final anecdotal bit of evidence: as participants planned their own program "graduation," this group of teenagers, given a choice of music for their party, chose patriotic American music.

Pamela Zeiser is an assistant professor in the department of political science and public administration at the University of North Florida.

ORDERING INFORMATION

ALL PRICES include shipping and handling (for orders outside the United States, please add $15 for shipping). National Civic League members receive a 10 percent discount. Bulk rates are available. See end of this list for ordering information.

Most Frequently Requested Publications

The Civic Index: A New Approach to Improving Community Life
  National Civic League staff, 1993
  50 pp., 7 × 10 paper, $7.00

The Community Visioning and Strategic Planning Handbook
  National Civic League staff, 1995
  53 pp., $23.00

Governance

National Report on Local Campaign Finance Reform
  New Politics Program staff, 1998
  96 pp., $15.00

Communities and the Voting Rights Act
  National Civic League staff, 1996
  118 pp., 8.5 × 11 paper, $12.00

Forms of Local Government
  National Civic League staff, 1993
  15 pp., 5.5 × 8.5 pamphlet, $3.00

Guide for Charter Commissions (Fifth Edition)
  National Civic League staff, 1991
  46 pp., 6 × 9 paper, $10.00

Handbook for Council Members in Council-Manager Cities (Fifth Edition)
  National Civic League staff, 1992
  38 pp., 6 × 9 paper, $12.00

Measuring City Hall Performance: Finally, A How-To Guide
  Charles K. Bens, 1991
  127 pp., 8.5 × 11 monograph, $15.00

Model County Charter (Revised Edition)
  National Civic League staff, 1990
  53 pp., 5.5 × 8.5 paper, $10.00

Modern Counties: Professional Management—The Non-Charter Route
  National Civic League staff, 1993
  54 pp., paper, $8.00

Term Limitations for Local Officials: A Citizen's Guide to Constructive Dialogue
  Laurie Hirschfeld Zeller, 1992
  24 pp., 5.5 × 8.5 pamphlet, $3.00

Using Performance Measurement in Local Government: A Guide to Improving Decisions, Performance, and Accountability
Paul D. Epstein, 1988
225 pp., 6 × 9 paper, $5.00

Model City Charter (Seventh Edition)
National Civic League staff, 1997
110 pp., 5.5 × 8.5 monograph, $14.00

Alliance for National Renewal

ANR Community Resource Manual
National Civic League Staff, 1996
80 pp., 8.5 × 11, $6.00

Taking Action: Building Communities That Strengthen Families
Special section in *Governing Magazine*, 1998
8 pp., 8.5 × 11 (color), $3.00

Communities That Strengthen Families
Insert in *Governing Magazine*, 1997
8 pp., 8.5 × 11 reprint, $3.00

Connecting Government and Neighborhoods
Insert in *Governing Magazine*, 1996
8 pp., 8.5 × 11 reprint, $3.00

The Culture of Renewal
Richard Louv, 1996
45 pp., $8.00

The Kitchen Table
Quarterly newsletter of Alliance for National Renewal, 1999
8 pp., annual subscription (4 issues) $12.00, free to ANR Partners

The Landscape of Civic Renewal
Civic renewal projects and studies from around the country, 1999
185 pp., $12.00

National Renewal
John W. Gardner, 1995
27 pp., 7 × 10, $7.00

San Francisco Civic Scan
Richard Louv, 1996
100 pp., $6.00

1998 Guide to the Alliance for National Renewal
National Civic League staff, 1998
50 pp., 4 × 9, $5.00

Springfield, Missouri: A Nice Community Wrestles with How to Become a Good Community
Alliance for National Renewal staff, 1996
13 pp., $7.00

Toward a Paradigm of Community-Making
  Allan Wallis, 1996
  60 pp., $12.00

The We Decade: Rebirth on Community
  Dallas Morning News, 1995
  39 pp., 8.5 × 14 reprint, $3.00

99 Things You Can Do for Your Community in 1999
  poster (folded), $6.00

Healthy Communities

Healthy Communities Handbook
  National Civic League staff, 1993
  162 pp., 8.5 × 11 monograph, $22.00

All-America City Awards

All-America City Yearbook (1991, 1992, 1993, 1994, 1995, 1996, 1997)
  National Civic League staff
  60 pp., 7 × 10 paper, $4.00 shipping and handling

All-America City Awards Audio Tape Briefing
  Audiotape, $4.00 shipping and handling

Diversity and Regionalism

Governance and Diversity:
Findings from Oakland, 1995
Findings from Fresno, 1995
Findings from Los Angeles, 1994
  National Civic League staff
  7 × 10 paper, $5.00 each

Networks, Trust and Values
  Allan D. Wallis, 1994
  51 pp., 7 × 10 paper, $7.00

Inventing Regionalism
  Allan D. Wallis, 1995
  75 pp., 8.5 × 11 monograph, $19.00

Leadership, Collaboration, and Community Building

Citistates: How Urban America Can Prosper in a Competitive World
  Neal Peirce, Curtis Johnson, and John Stuart Hall, 1993
  359 pp., 6.5 × 9.5, $25.00

Collaborative Leadership
  David D. Chrislip and Carl E. Larson, 1994
  192 pp., 6 × 9.5, $20.00

Good City and the Good Life
  Daniel Kemmis, 1995
  226 pp., 6 × 8.5, $23.00

On Leadership
  John W. Gardner, 1990
  220 pp., 6 × 9.5, $28.00

Politics for People: Finding a Responsible Public Voice
  David Mathews, 1994
  229 pp., 6 × 9.5, $20.00

Public Journalism and Public Life
  David "Buzz" Merritt, 1994
  129 pp., 6 × 9, $30.00

Resolving Municipal Disputes
  David Stiebel, 1992
  2 audiotapes and book, $15.00

Time Present, Time Past
  Bill Bradley, former chairman of the National Civic League, 1996
  450 pp., paper, $13.00

Transforming Politics
  David D. Chrislip, 1995
  12 pp., 7 × 10, $3.00

Revolution of the Heart
  Bill Shore, 1996
  167 pp., 8.5 × 5.75, $8.00

The Web of Life
  Richard Louv, 1996
  258 pp., 7.5 × 5.5, $15.00

Programs for Community Problem Solving

Systems Reform and Local Government: Improving Outcomes for Children, Families, and Neighborhoods
  1998, 47 pp., $12.00

Building Community: Exploring the Role of Social Capital and Local Government
  1998, 31 pp., $12.00

The Transformative Power of Governance: Strengthening Community Capacity to Improve Outcomes for Children, Families, and Neighborhoods
  1998, 33 pp., $12.00

Building the Collaborative Community
  Jointly published by the National Civic League and the National Institute for Dispute Resolution, 1994
  33 pp., $12.00

Negotiated Approaches to Environmental Decision Making in Communities: An Exploration of Lessons Learned
  Jointly published by the National Institute for Dispute Resolution and the Coalition to Improve Management in State and Local Government, 1996
  58 pp., $14.00

Community Problem Solving Case Summaries, Volume III
  1992, 52 pp., $19.00

Facing Racial and Cultural Conflicts: Tools for Rebuilding Community (Second Edition)
  1994, $24.00

Collaborative Transportation Planning Guidelines for Implementing ISTEA and the CAAA
  1993, 87 pp., $14.00

Collaborative Planning Video
  Produced by the American Planning Association, 1995
  6-hr. video and 46 pp. workshop materials, $103.00

Pulling Together: A Land Use and Development Consensus Building Manual
  A joint publication of PCPS and the Urban Land Institute, 1994
  145 pp., $34.00

Solving Community Problems by Consensus
  1990, 20 pp., $14.00

Involving Citizens in Community Decision Making: A Guidebook
  1992, 30 pp., $30.00

NATIONAL CIVIC LEAGUE sales policies: Orders must be paid in advance by check, VISA, or MasterCard. We are unable to process exchanges, returns, credits, or refunds. For orders outside the United States, add $15 for shipping.

TO PLACE AN ORDER:

CALL the National Civic League at (303) 571–4343 or (800) 223–6004, or

MAIL ORDERS TO:
  National Civic League
  1445 Market Street, Suite 300
  Denver, CO 80202–1717, or

E-MAIL the National Civic League at ncl@ncl.org